RESILIENCE THROUGH THE STORM

Johanne's Journey

Introduction: The Beginning of My Story

Life, as they say, has a habit of throwing us curveballs, hitting hardest when we least expect it. Growing up in West Yorkshire, in the little town of Silsden, I had no idea what life had in store for me. Those early years felt almost charmed—filled with warmth, laughter, and a closeness that only family can bring. My parents, Ted and Dena, made sure our home was a sanctuary of love and support. My sister Deborah, with her ever-gentle spirit, always had a kind word, and my brother Mark, though quiet, was a steady presence I could count on. Together, we were our own fortress.

But life doesn't give us guarantees. From a young age, I felt different. Learning didn't come easily to me, and those struggles made me stand out in ways I didn't want. The classroom became a place of battles, not just with books, but with the bullies who were quick to notice my vulnerabilities. Their words left scars, but they didn't define me. Even then, there was a spark within—a quiet, unbreakable determination to keep moving forward, no matter how many knocks I took.

At 26, my world was rocked by a cancer diagnosis, the first of many health challenges I never saw coming. Cancer came not just as a threat to my life, but as a test of my strength. It would have been enough for anyone to endure, yet it was just the beginning. Later, I faced the loss of my hearing, the loss of a kidney, and countless other hurdles that seemed insurmountable. Each one could have broken me, and I'd be lying if I said there weren't moments when I felt overwhelmed. But through it all, I clung to the belief that I could get through it, that I had something within me that even life's hardest blows couldn't take away.

This book is my journey—of love found and lost, of battles fought both inside and out, and of resilience that I never knew I had. I've walked through some dark valleys, yet here I am, on the other side, ready to share my story with you. My hope is that as you turn these pages, you'll find your own courage to face whatever life throws your way. Because if there's one thing I've learned, it's that resilience isn't something you're born with; it's something you find within yourself when you need it most.

So let this be my story, but also a reminder for you to keep going, to find your own strength, and to hold onto it, no matter what life brings

CHAPTERS

Chapter 1: "Roots of Strength"

Childhood, growing up in Silsden, the love and

protection of my family, the struggles of learning difficulties, and my close bond with my sister.

Chapter 2: "The Bully Within"

The bullying and mistreatment I endured growing up and how it shaped my trust issues. The emotional toll it took and how it impacted my relationships.

Chapter 3: "First Love, First Heartbreak"

My early relationships, my vulnerability, and how these shaped my emotional world and self-worth.

Chapter 4: "Marriage and Motherhood"

Meeting Stewart, becoming a mother to Adam, life on the farm, and the early days of my marriage.

Chapter 5: "The Weight of Responsibility"

Running the milk round, shouldering the burden of work as Stewart became less involved, balancing family life and being the breadwinner.

Chapter 6: "A Heart Attack's Ripple"

Stewart's heart attack and the strain it put on our marriage, work, and family. The beginning of cracks in our relationship.

Chapter 7: "The End of a Chapter"

Breaking up with Stewart, becoming a single mother, and navigating life without the stability of marriage.

Chapter 8: "Falling into Darkness"

Meeting Gary, his alcoholism, and the mental abuse I suffered. How this period marked a particularly low point in my life.

Chapter 9: "Adam's Rise, A Mother's Pride"

Despite everything, Adam's growth into a hardworking man with strong morals, my pride in him, and how his success gave me hope.

Chapter 10: "The Battle for My Body"

My first cancer diagnosis in my 20s, the fear and uncertainty, and how it affected me and my family.

Chapter 11: "Fighting Back Again"

The return of cancer 16 years later, the physical and emotional toll of having my breasts and ovaries removed. How I found the strength to keep going.

Chapter 12: "The Power of a Sister's Love"

My sister's unwavering support during my cancer journey and how losing her at the age of 48 shattered my world.

Chapter 13: "Rising from Grief"

Dealing with my sister's death and the immense grief, but also discovering my inner strength to move forward.

Chapter 14: "My Silent World"

Losing my hearing in my 30s, adjusting to life with hearing aids, and the emotional impact of living with this additional challenge.

Chapter 15: "Scarred but Beautiful"

The journey to accepting my body post-mastectomy, and the decision to get a tattoo to cover my scars as a symbol of survival.

Chapter 16: "Family Bonds"

The role my parents continue to play in my life, their wisdom and support, and my relationship with my brother despite the distance.

Chapter 17: "Transforming My Life"

My decision to focus on my health and the hard work that went into losing weight and regaining control of my body and life.

Chapter 18: "Resilience in Every Breath"

Where I am today: living alone but finding peace, strength, and pride in all I've overcome. A reflection on my life's lessons and the journey ahead.

Chapter 1: Roots of Strength

Silsden, a small town nestled in the rugged hills of West Yorkshire, is where my story begins. It's a place that lives and breathes with an unspoken strength. Rolling green hills stretch endlessly, marked by stone walls as old as the town itself, built to withstand time and weather alike.

The skies here are often a deep, brooding grey, a reflection of the tough and resilient people who call this place home. Life in Silsden is unembellished, as raw and real as the winds that sweep over the moors, yet within that rawness lies a unique beauty, something almost sacred. It was here, in the heart of this timeless landscape, that I learned about life, love, and survival.

My family didn't have much in the way of material wealth, but we were rich in what truly mattered. My father, Ted, was a man of few words but infinite strength. He worked long hours, his hands worn and calloused, building a life for us that we could rely on. His silence wasn't empty; it was full of resolve and dedication, a quiet but steady presence that held our family together.

When I think of integrity, I think of my father—his way of simply getting on with things, of enduring whatever came his way without complaint or self-pity. He was the rock upon which I built my understanding of resilience.

Then there was my mother, Dena. She was the heart of our home, a woman who filled our days with warmth and laughter. There was magic in the way she turned simple acts into love. A warm meal, a neatly folded shirt, the scent of bread baking in the oven—she wove love into our lives in a thousand little ways.

Her presence was as constant as the hills surrounding Silsden, grounding us all with her unshakeable kindness and patience. Whenever I felt the weight of the world bearing down, it was her gentle encouragement that lifted me up. She taught me that love, above all else, was the foundation upon which we could stand firm against life's tempests.

My sister, Deborah, was my closest friend and my protector. She was a few years older than me, and although she had her own dreams and friends, she always found time for me. Deborah had a warmth and understanding that few others possessed. She could sense my struggles without me saying a word, offering a hug or a smile that seemed to say, I see you, I understand. She was my shield against the world's harshness, always there to pull me close when things got too difficult. She became my constant, my beacon, my reminder that kindness could light even the darkest days.

My brother, Mark, was quieter, reserved in a way that made me feel like he was carrying his own battles. We weren't as close as Deborah and I were, but he had a way of being there when I needed him, a silent pillar of strength. I admired Mark, looked up to him from a distance, recognizing in him a quiet resilience that felt as old and grounded as the Yorkshire hills themselves. He was my reminder that sometimes strength isn't in loud words or grand gestures but in the quiet, steady determination to keep going, no matter what.

And then there was me, the youngest, the one who seemed to struggle where others glided through life. School was no easy place for a girl like me. I had learning difficulties that made each day feel like a battle I couldn't win.

Teachers tried to help, but often their efforts only highlighted my differences, making me feel like an outsider even in a room full of children. Children who, with the sharpness that only the young can wield, quickly sensed my struggles and made them the focus of their taunts. Bullying began as whispered jabs and mocking glances but soon escalated, each taunt chipping away at my confidence. They called me "stupid," "slow," words that burrowed deep, planting seeds of doubt that would take years to uproot.

It was a painful existence, caught between the warmth of home and the cruelty of the outside world. I became withdrawn, my voice growing softer, my laughter more guarded. The world outside felt hostile, a place that didn't understand me, didn't want to. I was left questioning my own worth, wondering if I would ever truly belong. But every day, I would come home to my family—a haven that wrapped around me like a soft, protective cloak. I could walk through our front door, and there would be Deborah's smile, my mother's open arms, my father's steady presence. They saw beyond the labels, beyond the struggles, seeing in me the strength I couldn't yet recognize.

In those early years, I came to understand that my family was not just a support system—they were my foundation, the roots from which I drew strength. My father taught me resilience through his silent endurance, my mother taught me love's transformative power, and Deborah showed me the value of kindness, even when the world offered none in return. Mark, though distant, reminded me that sometimes the greatest strength lies in quiet, steady perseverance.

The bullying, the struggles with learning, the feelings of isolation—they were painful, yes, but they were also shaping me, strengthening me. They forced me to look inward, to find a core of resilience nurtured by my family's love and belief in me. Each cruel word, each challenge, was building within me a foundation of strength, resilience, and understanding. I didn't know it then, but those experiences would become the building blocks of a life lived with purpose, a life that would teach me that true strength lies not in fitting in but in standing firm in who you are.

The love and lessons my family imparted in those early years became my compass, guiding me through the storms yet to come. They taught me that the world may not always be kind, but there is power in facing it with kindness. They showed me that true worth isn't found in others' opinions but in one's own sense of purpose and resilience. And above all, they gave me the courage to keep going, to embrace the journey, no matter how rocky the road or dark the path.

In the roots of Silsden, the heart of my family, and the hardships of those early years, I found my strength. And as I would later discover, that strength—like the hills and walls of Yorkshire—was steadfast, ready to withstand the winds of life's fiercest storms.

Chapter 2: The Bully Within

The walk to school was short, yet to me, it sometimes felt like miles stretched out before me, each step heavy with dread. Silsden, with its familiar cobbled streets, had once seemed like a sanctuary, a place wrapped in warmth and the comfort of familiarity. But school—school was different. It was a place where a child like me didn't fit, where every struggle was laid bare under the unforgiving gaze of teachers and classmates alike.

Back in the 1970s, children like me—those who couldn't sit still, who questioned everything, whose minds wandered down paths unknown—were labeled "troublemakers" or "disruptive." Words like "learning disability" or "attention issues" hadn't yet made their way into classrooms, and if they had, nobody spoke of them. Instead, children like me were expected to conform, to learn without help, to somehow keep pace in a world that constantly felt just out of reach.

As I sat in those cold, unforgiving classrooms, I felt the weight of my "difference" pressing on me like a heavy, unshakeable coat. There I was, a girl with a head full of questions, thoughts racing faster than I could understand, and a spirit that ached to run free. But the classroom was a place of stillness, of order, where eyes watched me with a mix of frustration and impatience. A teacher would ask a question, and I'd hesitate, wondering if my answer would sound "right." And when it didn't, their looks of frustration only deepened, as if my missteps were an inconvenience rather than a plea for understanding.

Some teachers dismissed me with sighs and curt remarks, their expectations already low, as if they'd long since decided I was just "one of those children." Others simply ignored me, and in a way, that was worse. I'd stare at the blackboard, the words blurring and tangling together, my mind lost in a fog that I didn't know how to clear. No one ever asked why I struggled—they only saw the struggle itself.

My classmates saw it too, and children, they have a way of sensing weakness, of sniffing out the smallest difference and turning it into something cruel. I don't remember every detail; time has mercifully blurred many of those moments. But the feelings, those I remember—the unease, the fear, the growing sense of isolation as I realized I didn't fit in. The names they called me stung like nettles, small yet sharp, lodging deep in my mind. Sometimes, they'd laugh, and I'd wonder what was so funny, only to realize it was me.

There was one afternoon I remember clearly, perhaps because it hurt the most. I was sitting in the classroom, trying to focus on my sums. The teacher had asked the class a question, and a hand shot up, but it wasn't to answer. It was to point, to laugh. "She can't even read right!" the girl said with a sneer. Her words felt like a slap, not only because they were untrue but because I sensed the judgment behind them—the belief that I was somehow less, somehow broken.

It was easier to retreat, to stay quiet, to slip to the back of the classroom where I could observe without drawing attention. I learned to keep my head down, to avoid eye contact, and to sink into my own world. But no matter how hard I tried, the taunts and whispers followed me, echoing louder in my mind than any lesson being taught. They grew into something larger, a voice in my own head that whispered I wasn't good enough, that I wasn't like the others, that something in me was flawed.

Home became my refuge, the one place where the harshness of the outside world couldn't touch me. My parents, Ted and Dena, didn't know the full extent of my struggles—I couldn't bring myself to tell them. But somehow, they sensed it. My mother would brush a gentle hand over my head or linger by my side at the dinner table, offering comfort without words. My father, a man of few but carefully chosen words, would sometimes say, "You're strong, Johanne. Don't let anyone tell you otherwise."

But it was my sister, Deborah, who became my true shield. Deborah, with her easy smile and unshakable loyalty, who would sit beside me in the quiet of my room, reading or simply being there. She didn't need to ask questions; she already seemed to know the answers. In her presence, I felt understood, valued, even loved for the very things that others saw as flaws. "They don't see you like I do," she'd whisper. "You're brilliant, Johanne, just in your own way."

Still, the bullying left its mark. I began to view myself through the eyes of those who tormented me, seeing not a girl full of dreams and curiosity, but a clumsy outsider, unworthy of acceptance. Friendships felt like distant dreams, and I guarded myself, building walls of silence and solitude. If I didn't open up, then they couldn't hurt me. Or so I thought.

School assemblies would sometimes bring up the notion of kindness, of treating others with respect. But those words, meant to uplift, felt hollow to me. The children who needed those lessons most were the ones who sneered and mocked as I sat, shrinking into myself, hoping to go unnoticed. Teachers, despite their intentions, seemed oblivious to the struggles of children like me, who didn't fit the mold, who existed in spaces no one wanted to understand.

It would be years before I came to understand that my struggles were not a sign of failure but of differences that no one had yet learned to embrace. I wasn't "slow" or "difficult," as I'd been labeled—I was simply wired to see the world differently. But in that moment, all I knew was the overwhelming desire to escape, to fade into the background where no one could see or judge me.

As time went on, I came to realize that the walls I had built around myself were as much a prison as a refuge. The voice in my head—the bully I had internalized—needed to be silenced. Slowly, I began to replace those hurtful words with ones of kindness, to tell myself I was enough, just as I was. It was a slow process, like chipping away at stone, but over time, I began to rebuild myself from within.

Looking back, I see those years as ones of pain, yes, but also of growth. They taught me resilience, compassion, and the ability to see beyond the surface. My struggles, once a source of shame, became a foundation on which I built a new understanding of myself. I learned to rise above, to find my voice, and to become the person I had once needed in those dark days.

In sharing my story, I hope to reach others who have walked a similar path, who have felt the sting of isolation and the weight of being different. To them, I say this: You are not alone. You are not defined by the names others may call you or the struggles you face. You are more than the sum of your hardships. You are strong, resilient, and worthy of love and understanding. And in time, you will see that every scar, every setback, has made you who you are—a person of strength and beauty beyond measure.

Chapter 3: First Love, First Heartbreak

Stepping into my teenage years felt like venturing into a new world, a world where everything felt heightened, intense, and alive with possibilities I could barely comprehend. Silsden, with its quiet streets and familiar faces, seemed to change before my eyes, transforming from a safe haven into a place of endless wonder, uncertainty, and, at times, deep longing. It was during these formative years that I encountered my first taste of love —a whirlwind of emotions that brought me soaring heights of joy, only to come crashing down into the depths of heartache.

I first met Kevin on a blustery autumn morning when we were paired together for a school project. He was quick-witted, with dark hair that fell carelessly over his brow and an easy, confident smile that could make anyone feel at ease. Popular

RESILIENCE THROUGH THE STORM

and effortlessly charming, Kevin seemed to embody everything I felt I wasn't: bold, assured, and wholly unburdened by the doubts and insecurities that haunted me. He moved through the world with an ease I could only dream of, and yet, for reasons I couldn't fathom, he seemed to be interested in me.

As we worked together, Kevin's kindness began to chip away at my guarded exterior. He listened to me in a way that felt sincere, laughed at my jokes, and asked questions that made me feel, perhaps for the first time, truly seen. I found myself looking forward to our study sessions, feeling a warmth in my chest every time he smiled at me, a feeling that was both exhilarating and terrifying. I didn't fully understand it, but I knew it was special, something new and fragile that I wanted to protect.

When Kevin asked me to the school dance, my heart nearly burst with joy. The idea of being wanted, of stepping into that room on his arm, made me feel as though I'd shed my insecurities and emerged as someone beautiful, someone who mattered. I spent hours preparing, choosing a dress that shimmered in the light, hoping it would help me capture even a sliver of the confidence that seemed to radiate from Kevin so naturally.

The dance was everything I'd hoped it would be. We twirled under the dim lights, laughing and talking as if no one else existed. For those few hours, I felt untouchable, wrapped in a blissful bubble where my worries seemed miles away. I felt like I was floating, lifted by a happiness I hadn't known I could feel. But like so many fleeting moments of joy, it couldn't last forever.

As the days went by, my insecurities started to creep back in, clouding my newfound confidence with shadows of doubt. I'd been haunted for so long by the belief that I was somehow "less"—less confident, less capable, less deserving. Every small silence, every subtle shift in Kevin's attention, felt magnified, like proof that he was losing interest, that I wasn't enough. I tried to bury these fears, telling myself I was overthinking, but they gnawed at me, growing louder with each passing day.

One afternoon, in a moment of weakness, I asked Kevin if he really liked me. The question slipped out before I could stop it, raw and vulnerable. His reaction was one of confusion; he reassured me, but I could sense the distance beginning to grow between us. I wanted so badly to believe him, but the voice of doubt was louder than his reassurances, whispering that this happiness was too fragile to last.

In the following weeks, Kevin's warmth seemed to cool, replaced by a polite indifference that stung more than any outright rejection. He stopped meeting me between classes, offered half-hearted excuses for missed meet-ups, and avoided my gaze when we crossed paths. The certainty I'd once felt in his presence was replaced by a gnawing ache, a dread that seemed to settle in my chest and weigh me down.

The final blow came in the form of a whispered conversation I overheard. A mutual friend mentioned that Kevin had started seeing someone else—a girl who was everything I wasn't: outgoing, confident, with an ease that I could only envy from afar. It felt as though my world shattered in that moment, each piece a painful reminder of the inadequacies I believed defined me. Heartbreak became a weight I couldn't escape, a constant reminder of the fragile nature of the happiness I'd tasted.

In the days that followed, I withdrew even further into myself. I walked the familiar streets of Silsden feeling like a ghost, haunted by memories of what could have been. My mind replayed every moment with Kevin, searching for where I'd gone wrong, convinced that if I'd just been better, more confident, less "me," things might have turned out differently. It was a spiral of self-doubt and regret that seemed impossible to escape, each thought a thorn that dug deeper into my wounded heart.

But amid the darkness, there was Deborah, my sister and my constant. She'd sit beside me, offering quiet comfort, her hand warm and steady in mine. "You're worth so much more than this, Johanne," she'd say, her voice a soothing balm for my battered spirit. "One day, someone will see you the way I do, and they'll love you for exactly who you are." Her faith in me was unwavering, a light that guided me through the storm, reminding me that this heartbreak, as crushing as it felt, did not define my worth.

In time, I began to see the truth in Deborah's words. This experience, painful as it was, taught me that my value wasn't dependent on someone else's approval. I threw myself into activities that brought me joy, rediscovering the parts of myself that had been overshadowed by my insecurities. Painting, writing, and volunteering filled my days, each new pursuit a step towards reclaiming my sense of self. I realized that my worth was intrinsic, rooted in who I was, not in who loved me or didn't.

Healing was a journey, a process that required me to rebuild the trust I'd lost not only in others but in myself. I learned that vulnerability, though it opened me to the possibility of hurt, was also a source of strength. It was a reminder that love, even when it ended in heartbreak, had the power to shape me, to teach me, to guide me toward a truer understanding of myself.

As the seasons changed and time softened the edges of my pain, I found myself ready to open my heart again, albeit with a newfound caution and wisdom. Each friendship, each budding connection, became an opportunity to rewrite my story, to love in a way that didn't compromise who I was. I discovered that true love wasn't about losing myself in someone else, but about finding a shared space where I could be fully me.

Looking back, my first love, though it ended in heartbreak,

left me with a precious gift: the understanding that I was enough, that I was worthy of love, not in spite of my perceived flaws, but because of them. Each scar, each lingering ache, became a testament to my resilience, a reminder that I could survive, heal, and emerge stronger.

This chapter of my life, once filled with innocence and pain, taught me a valuable truth: love, even when it falters, has the power to transform us. It teaches us not only about others but about our own capacity to endure, to grow, and to find strength within ourselves. And with that realization, I found peace, ready to greet the future with hope, courage, and a heart open to whatever lay ahead.

Chapter 4: Marriage and Motherhood

The memories of my wedding to Stewart feel like flashes, half-remembered and hazy, as though seen through a veil. I remember Silsden's St. James Church with its grand stone arches, the smell of fresh flowers and the hum of voices, friends and family gathered from all over. And though I can't recall the exact moment he proposed, the wedding itself stands out, bright as day, a tapestry of joy woven with the threads of everyone's love and well-wishes.

On that chilly morning, I found myself transformed in a wedding dress that shimmered like moonlight, a beautiful creation that flowed with every step. My hair was braided and adorned with delicate flowers, and as I stood in front of the mirror, a wave of emotions washed over me—excitement, nerves, and a quiet joy that made my heart flutter. Family and friends filled the old stone church, each one there to celebrate not just a union but the intertwining of lives and dreams.

The pews were packed, and the murmur of voices seemed to blend with the creaking of the wooden floor as people shifted in their seats, eagerly awaiting the ceremony. When the doors opened, and I walked down the aisle, the gentle light streaming through the stained-glass windows caught the sparkles of my dress. Stewart stood at the altar, looking as though he, too, had been transformed by the occasion, his eyes reflecting the same mixture of excitement and tenderness that filled my own heart. There was a strength to him, a solidity that calmed me, and in that moment, I felt the gravity of the vows we were about to exchange.

The ceremony passed like a dream. My heart beat faster as we spoke our promises to one another, each word feeling as sacred as the ground we stood upon. As Stewart slipped the ring onto my finger, I felt a warmth, a connection that seemed to bind us together not just in that moment, but in every moment that would follow. The church filled with laughter and applause as we were pronounced husband and wife, our families joining in the celebration with joyful shouts and embraces.

After the ceremony, we stepped outside into the brisk autumn air, where our loved ones surrounded us with hugs and laughter. The church bells rang out, their echoes bouncing off the old stone walls and filling the village with a sound that felt as ancient as the hills themselves. We moved to the reception, where tables were set with simple, home-cooked meals, and the air was filled with the sound of music and laughter, family and friends sharing stories, love, and food, their spirits as warm as the glow from the candles that dotted each table.

Life after the wedding settled into a steady rhythm as Stewart and I found our footing as a married couple. We moved into a small farmhouse just outside of town, nestled between fields that stretched to the horizon, with only the distant mountains to mark where the sky met the land. I spent my days learning the rhythms of farm life, managing the household, and supporting Stewart as he poured his heart into the land.

Soon, we were blessed with news of a new addition to our family. The discovery that I was pregnant filled us with joy and nervous anticipation. We spent countless evenings talking about our dreams for this new life, planning out the nursery, and wondering who this little person would become. When Adam was born, he brought with him a light that filled every corner of our lives. Holding him for the first time, I felt a love that was fierce and protective, a love that made every hardship feel insignificant.

But as the years passed, the challenges of farm life grew. Stewart's long hours on the land took a toll on him, and I often found myself alone, balancing the responsibilities of motherhood with the demands of the farm. Adam's needs and my own dreams began to clash with the daily demands of a life rooted in such hard labor. Though I cherished every moment with my family, there were times when I yearned for something more, a part of myself that seemed to have been lost in the whirlwind of marriage and motherhood.

In those quiet moments, when the house was finally still and the day's work was done, I would sit by the window, looking out at the fields stretching endlessly into the night. There, in the solitude, I found space to reconnect with myself, to dream of possibilities beyond the boundaries of our life on the farm. Yet, despite the yearnings that tugged at my heart, I couldn't ignore the love that bound us together—the love that had first sparked in that crowded pub and blossomed in the walls of St. James Church.

As Adam grew, his laughter and curiosity filled our days with purpose. Stewart would take him out to the fields, teaching him about the land, passing down the knowledge that had been instilled in him since he was a boy. Their bond was strong, a reflection of the love Stewart felt for his family and his deep connection to the land.

And so, we continued, our lives woven together by the threads of love, resilience, and shared dreams. Despite the struggles and uncertainties, I felt rooted in a life that, though challenging, was rich in its simplicity and deep in its joys. Looking back now, I see that our marriage, with its unspoken promises and shared silences, became the foundation upon which we built our family. It was a love that didn't need grand gestures or perfect moments, but a love that endured, growing stronger with each passing season.

Chapter 5: The Weight of Responsibility

The milk round began not as a choice, but as a necessity—a lifeline after everything else fell apart. When foot-and-mouth disease spread through our part of the country, it didn't just take livestock; it took people's livelihoods, leaving farms empty and families wondering what to do next. Stewart lost his job, and with it, the land and the life he'd devoted himself to. The farm that had once been the heart of our world became a ghost, a painful reminder of everything he'd poured his soul into, only to see it swept away. We moved into a small house in town, and as much as we tried to look forward, the loss lingered, heavy in the air.

It was then, during those desperate days of trying to rebuild from nothing, that the milk round came along. It wasn't glamorous, and it wasn't what we'd dreamed of, but it was a way to survive. For Stewart, though, it seemed a poor substitute for the life he had known. I could see the change in him; the spark that once drove him through early mornings and hard, honest labor was dimmed, replaced by a quiet weariness I didn't know how to touch. He came along on the milk round, mostly to sit behind the wheel of the van, a silent companion who watched the world go by with a distant gaze. Every so often, he'd help with the crates, lifting bottles to the doors or smiling at familiar faces, but his heart wasn't in it. It was like he'd left a part of himself back on that farm.

The milk round quickly became my responsibility, though I hadn't anticipated how much it would take to keep it going. Those first few weeks were a whirlwind, as I juggled not just the demands of delivering milk, but also the full weight of motherhood and keeping our home running. Stewart's detachment left me carrying the burden alone, though I tried to pretend that everything was as it should be.

Each morning started before dawn, when the sky was still cloaked in darkness and the town lay silent. Adam, my young son, would rise early too, rubbing the sleep from his eyes as he came downstairs to help. I'd try to shoo him back to bed, insisting he needed his rest for school, but he'd only shake his head and get to work alongside me. He was barely old enough to shoulder such responsibilities, yet he handled them with a quiet determination that broke and warmed my heart all at once. Together, we'd load the crates into the van, bottles clinking in the cold as we prepared for the route ahead.

As the round grew, we needed extra hands to keep up with the deliveries. I found two young lads who were eager for the work, bringing with them a burst of energy and laughter that lifted the mornings. They'd joke and tease as they loaded the crates, swapping stories and keeping spirits high even on the toughest days. With them, the milk round became something more than just a job; it became a small community. Our shared effort, the familiar faces we saw each morning, and the routines we built together made those early starts feel a little less lonely.

Still, I felt the strain of carrying so much on my own. Stewart would sit in the van, his face turned away from the others, watching the streets go by in silence. At times, I'd catch his eye, hoping for a smile, a flicker of the man I'd married, but he remained distant. I longed to reach him, to find a way through the walls he'd built around himself, but it felt like trying to grasp smoke. In moments of quiet, when the deliveries slowed, I would ask him if he was alright, if there was anything I could do, but he would only nod and look away, his spirit tucked deep where I couldn't follow.

In his absence, the lads and I grew closer. They became my allies, helping me carry the weight Stewart had once shared with me. They took pride in their work, going the extra mile to make sure every customer was served with a smile and that each bottle found its rightful place. Their cheer was infectious, and on good days, I'd find myself laughing along with them, reminded that even in hardship, there could be moments of joy. These young men, Adam, and our customers became my lifeline, each one a reminder that I wasn't as alone as I felt.

There was an undeniable satisfaction in the work, a sense of accomplishment each morning when the last delivery was done, and the crates stood empty in the back of the van. I'd return home weary, yet filled with a quiet pride that kept me going. Adam would often join me for a cup of tea before he left for school, his face bright with the satisfaction of having helped. His steady presence, his willingness to step up when we needed him, became a source of strength I could always count on. He didn't complain, and he didn't falter, despite the demands we placed on him. He was the best part of every morning, the light that made those dark, early hours bearable.

With each passing week, the milk round continued to expand, our little business reaching more people and creating new connections. I found a sense of purpose in those early starts, those chilly mornings, and the simple act of bringing fresh milk to people's doorsteps. Our customers became familiar faces, people who counted on us to show up, rain or shine. Some of them knew about Stewart's struggle, his quiet withdrawal, and would give me a nod of understanding or offer words of encouragement that kept me going when I felt ready to collapse under the weight of it all.

But the strain wasn't just on my shoulders. Stewart's silence grew heavier, his health visibly suffering under the weight of whatever burden he carried. I would sometimes hear him coughing in the quiet of the night, or catch him clutching his chest, though he'd brush it off, assuring me it was nothing. I wanted to press him to open up, to tell me what lay on his heart, but he held it all in, keeping his pain locked away where even I couldn't reach.

Looking back, I see how those years wore on us both. The milk round had become a lifeline, yes, but it was also a strain, a relentless demand that pulled us in opposite directions. I poured myself into the work, taking pride in every delivery, every satisfied customer, while Stewart seemed to sink deeper into himself. There were nights when I would sit beside him in silence, hoping he'd share what weighed on his mind, but he'd only pat my hand, a faint smile flickering across his face before fading away.

And then, just as the routine had become almost second nature, the unthinkable happened.

Chapter 6: A Heart Attack's Ripple

The day Stewart had his heart attack is a memory that lingers like a shadow—a day when life changed in an instant, leaving us scrambling to make sense of what was left. It began like any other workday. We had just finished the milk round, the early morning rush that took us across town to deliver milk to families who had come to rely on us. My parents had come for a visit that morning, bringing a warm energy to the house that felt like a blessing. We gathered in the kitchen, the smell of coffee and toast filling the air, everyone in good spirits after the hard work was done.

As we settled into the warmth of the kitchen, Stewart slipped outside for a quick smoke, his usual ritual after the morning's deliveries. We barely took notice; it was a habit as familiar as breathing. But after a few minutes passed, my mother glanced toward the back door, her brow furrowed in concern.

"Stewart's been a while, hasn't he?" she said casually, though there was a hint of worry in her voice.

I looked up, shrugging off the thought at first. "Probably just enjoying the fresh air," I said, not thinking much of it.

But when Stewart didn't return, my mum's concern grew. She turned to Adam, who was already halfway to the door, curious about what might be keeping his dad. "Go and check on him, love," she urged. Adam nodded, stepping outside with the nonchalance of a young boy used to seeing his dad take his time with a cigarette.

Moments later, Adam rushed back in, his face pale and eyes wide with fear. He looked at my mum, his voice trembling. "Gran… I don't know how to say it, but Dad's holding his chest, and… he looks green."

My mother's face turned to alarm. Without hesitation, she said, "He's having a heart attack." Her words cut through the air, sharp and certain. I froze, my mind struggling to catch up, while my mother sprang into action, grabbing the phone and dialing for an ambulance. Her voice, normally warm and calm, was urgent as she spoke to the operator, relaying our address and Stewart's condition with a steady resolve that I couldn't summon in that moment.

I stumbled toward the door, a cold dread settling into my bones as I rushed outside. There he was—Stewart, leaning against the wall, his hand clutched tightly over his chest, his face drained of all color. He looked at me, his eyes wide with fear, and I felt my own heart lurch at the sight. I'd never seen him like this, never imagined this strong, steady man brought so low.

The wait for the ambulance felt endless. My mother stayed by the phone, coordinating with the paramedics, while I knelt beside Stewart, holding his hand and murmuring words I barely remember now, something to keep him anchored, to keep him with me. Adam stood nearby, his face etched with a fear no child should ever have to feel, and I reached for him, pulling him close, grounding myself in the warmth of his presence.

Finally, the ambulance arrived, and the paramedics moved quickly, assessing Stewart's condition and stabilizing him for transport. I wanted to go with him, to be there every step of the way, but the paramedics insisted I stay back, giving him space to breathe. I watched the ambulance pull away, my heart heavy with worry and fear. For the first time in my life, I felt utterly helpless, watching the man I loved be driven away, not knowing what would come next.

The hours that followed were a blur of phone calls, anxious waiting, and whispered prayers. My parents stayed close, offering comfort in their steady way, their presence a lifeline as I grappled with the terrifying unknown. I kept looking at Adam, seeing the worry etched across his young face, and tried to put on a brave front, though inside, I felt like a child myself, terrified and uncertain.

When the doctor finally called, his tone was measured but cautious. Stewart had indeed suffered a heart attack, and though he was stable for the moment, his recovery would be a long, uncertain road. Relief washed over me, tempered by the knowledge that our lives were about to change in ways I couldn't yet fully grasp. The road ahead was shrouded in questions, each one more daunting than the last.

The days that followed felt surreal. Stewart was weak and quiet, his spirit dulled by the trauma of what he'd been through. When he finally came home, I felt a fragile hope, tempered by the weight of new responsibilities that had only just begun to settle on my shoulders. Our roles had shifted dramatically, and though we had faced challenges together before, this was different. This was a test of endurance, patience, and a strength I wasn't sure I possessed.

Stewart struggled to adjust, the toll of his heart attack evident in his every movement. Gone was the energetic man who once tackled each day with a quiet resolve; in his place was someone who looked at life with a newfound weariness. Tasks that once came easily now seemed insurmountable, and the frustration of his limitations often spilled over in sharp words and tense silences. I tried to be patient, to remind myself that he was healing in his own way, but the strain on our relationship was undeniable. The life we had known felt distant, replaced by a fragile existence that neither of us quite understood.

As Stewart grappled with his recovery, the responsibility of the milk round fell solely on me. I had always helped, of course, but now it was up to me to keep it running smoothly, to manage the orders, the deliveries, and every detail that kept our business afloat. Adam, bless him, stepped up to help in every way he could. He'd rise early each morning, rubbing the sleep from his eyes, his small hands reaching for crates that seemed far too heavy for him. He'd come along on the route, lifting bottles with a quiet determination that broke my heart and filled me with pride all at once.

We worked side by side, mother and son, navigating each day's demands with a resilience I hadn't known we possessed. The milk round grew over time, and soon we had two young lads helping us, easing the burden that had once seemed overwhelming. Their energy brought a fresh spark to our mornings, a reminder that even in hardship, there could be laughter, camaraderie, and a sense of purpose.

But despite the support, the weight of responsibility was relentless. I carried not only the physical demands of the milk round but also the emotional strain of supporting Stewart through his recovery. Each evening, after the day's work was done, I would collapse into bed, my body exhausted, my mind racing with worry for the future. Stewart remained withdrawn, a shadow of the man I had married, and I longed to reach him, to find a way to bridge the silence that had grown between us.

One night, as I sat at the kitchen table, buried in paperwork and bills, Stewart shuffled into the room, his face lined with fatigue. He looked at me for a long moment, his gaze heavy with unspoken words. I felt my throat tighten, a surge of emotion rising within me, and I finally spoke the words that had been building inside me for so long.

"Stewart, we can't go on like this," I said, my voice trembling. "I need you... Adam needs you. We need to face this together."

He looked away, his shoulders slumped, and for a moment, I thought he might walk away, retreat back into his own world. But then he nodded, his gaze meeting mine with a glimmer of the man I remembered. "I know," he whispered. "I've been lost... but I'm here, Johanne. I'm trying."

In that quiet moment, something shifted. The weight of the heart attack, the fear and uncertainty, all the unspoken words —they began to lift, just a little. We weren't healed, and the road ahead remained steep and uncertain, but for the first time in what felt like forever, I felt a flicker of hope.

The heart attack had sent a ripple through our lives, challenging everything we thought we knew. But it had also brought us closer, forcing us to confront the fragility of life and the strength we found in each other. Together, we faced the days with a newfound resilience, knowing that while life would never be the same, we would move forward—side by side, one step at a time.

Chapter 7: The End of a Chapter

Twenty years. Two decades spent building a life, raising
a child, and weaving dreams together. When Stewart and
I first married, I thought we'd be together forever—that
we'd grow old side by side, looking back on a life filled with
shared memories and laughter. But life, as it often does,
took us down paths we couldn't have foreseen, and over
the years, we found ourselves moving further apart, until
eventually, there was little left of the bond we once shared.

As the years passed, our marriage slowly transformed. The
laughter that once filled our home grew quieter, replaced by
unspoken tensions and unmet expectations. We had become
different people, each shaped by our experiences, our own
struggles, and the quiet dreams that, in some ways, began to
pull us apart. For the sake of Adam, though, we continued on,
determined to give him the stability we both knew he deserved.
We put up a united front, concealing the growing cracks in our
relationship, not wanting him to feel the weight of our struggles.

The years blurred together in a rhythm of work, parenting,
and routine, but the gap between us widened. It was as if we
were living parallel lives, crossing paths out of duty rather
than connection. The love that had once bound us felt like
a distant memory, a ghost of a promise we had both tried
to keep but could no longer hold onto. We'd sit across from
each other in silence, each wrapped in our own thoughts,
knowing that the closeness we once shared was lost.

When Adam turned eighteen, something shifted within me.
He was now a young man, capable of forging his own path, and
I felt a deep need to reclaim the part of myself that had been

lost over the years. Stewart and I had built a life together, but as Adam prepared to step into adulthood, I began to see our lives more clearly, unclouded by the necessity to hold onto a marriage that no longer brought joy or companionship. It was time to face the truth that our journey together had reached its end.

But I didn't want to make a decision that would leave Adam feeling abandoned or torn. He had been a witness to our life, to the struggles and the quiet heartaches, and I knew he likely sensed more than we'd ever acknowledged. So, one quiet evening, I sat down with him, my heart pounding as I prepared to explain what had been stirring within me.

"Adam," I began, my voice steady but soft, "I need to talk to you about something important. Your dad and I… we're thinking about going our separate ways."

He looked at me, his eyes thoughtful, and for a moment, I felt like he was the one comforting me. "I understand, Mum," he said, his voice calm but tinged with a quiet sadness. "I've seen how things have been between you and Dad. You both deserve to be happy."

The relief that washed over me was overwhelming. His blessing felt like permission to finally take a step I had been considering for years. We hugged, and as I held him close, I felt a surge of gratitude for the young man he had become—wise, compassionate, and strong enough to handle this change.

When I shared my decision with Stewart, it was as though we both released a breath we had been holding for years. We had come to this place together, and while the parting was painful, there was a mutual understanding that this was necessary, that our paths were no longer meant to run alongside each other. We spoke quietly, without blame or anger, acknowledging the love that had once been there but accepting that it was no longer enough to keep us bound together.

In the days that followed, the reality of the separation settled in. The house felt strangely empty, as though it, too, was mourning the end of our family as we knew it. There were moments of doubt, flashes of sadness, and even guilt, wondering if we could have done more, held on longer. But each time I felt myself slipping into regret, I reminded myself that this decision was about more than just ending a marriage; it was about stepping into a life where I could find joy and purpose again, unburdened by the weight of a love that had long faded.

Stewart moved out first, and though it was an amicable departure, the sight of him packing up his belongings stirred memories of the life we had built together, piece by piece. I watched him load the last of his things into his car, and as he drove away, I felt a bittersweet mix of relief and sorrow. He had been my partner, my friend, and the father of my child. I knew I would always care for him, but our lives had diverged in ways that no amount of compromise could mend.

Adam, ever the gentle soul, provided support in a way that felt beyond his years. He would sit with me during quiet evenings, sharing stories or simply listening, giving me the space to grieve the end of one chapter while embracing the beginning of another. I knew this separation was as much a change for him as it was for me, but his strength, his willingness to understand, reminded me that we would be okay, that we could forge a new kind of family, one built on love, honesty, and acceptance.

With Stewart gone, I began to create a new rhythm for myself, a life that was entirely my own. I redecorated the house, filling it with colors and objects that brought me joy, that felt like an expression of the person I was rediscovering. Each small change, each touch of warmth and personality, felt like a reclamation of myself, a way to shed the sadness of the past and welcome the possibility of new beginnings.

For the first time in years, I felt a sense of freedom—a chance to rediscover my own dreams, to reconnect with friends, to try new things without the shadow of a strained marriage hanging over me. I enrolled in community classes, found joy in volunteering, and began nurturing interests that had long been set aside. It was a slow process, but with each day, I felt myself growing stronger, more grounded, and more at peace.

Evenings with Adam became a treasured ritual, our time to talk, to share our thoughts and dreams. He spoke of his own plans, his hopes for the future, and I saw a fire in him that reminded me of myself when I was young—a spark of ambition and curiosity. We encouraged each other, finding strength in our shared journey, our bond deepening as we navigated this new chapter together.

In the months that followed, I realized that ending my marriage was not just about parting from Stewart; it was about coming home to myself. It was about shedding the weight of a love that had turned into duty and reclaiming my right to happiness, to fulfillment, to a life where I could be fully present. There were days when the loneliness crept in, when I missed the companionship that marriage had once brought, but those moments grew fewer, replaced by a quiet confidence that I had made the right choice.

Looking back, I see that the end of my marriage to Stewart was both an ending and a beginning. It was a necessary step in my journey, a way to honor the life we had shared while giving myself the freedom to move forward. I no longer saw the separation as a failure but as a courageous decision to seek a life that was true to me, a life that allowed me to be the best version of myself.

The love Stewart and I had shared would always be a part of me, woven into the fabric of my life, but it no longer defined me. I was more than just a wife or mother; I was a woman standing at the threshold of a new chapter, a chapter filled with possibility, growth, and the promise of rediscovery. And as I embraced that future, I held onto the lessons of my past, knowing that each experience, each heartache, had brought me closer to the person I was meant to become.

Chapter 8: Falling into Darkness

When my marriage to Stewart ended, I was filled with both relief and a deep, gnawing apprehension. I knew the life I had chosen would not be easy; it meant standing on my own, a single mother to Adam, and finding a way to build a new path. For a while, I was hopeful, almost naïve in my optimism that life would bring us happiness again.

Then I met Gary. He entered my world like a storm, full of intensity and excitement. He was different from Stewart—he had a carefree, impulsive side that made me feel alive, as if I had broken free from an invisible cage. Gary brought with him laughter, a lightness, and a confidence that drew me in like a magnet. And though I had only just begun to heal, I let him in. For the first time in a long time, I felt seen and wanted.

In those early days, Gary seemed everything I thought I needed. We spent hours talking, sharing dreams I'd long buried, and he encouraged me to believe in the possibility of a new life, of happiness. But as the weeks turned into months, small cracks began to show. What had felt like harmless fun—a drink here, a late night there—soon became a ritual, a steady descent into the kind of drinking that wasn't just for enjoyment. Before I knew it, Gary's warmth turned cold, his laughter replaced by sullen silence, or worse, biting words that left scars as deep as any wound.

Adam watched the transformation with a cautious eye. At 18, he was no longer a child, yet his world had been shaken enough by my split from Stewart. He wanted to see me happy, I think, but in Gary, he sensed the danger that I couldn't, or perhaps wouldn't, see. I told myself he didn't understand, that he just wanted his mother all to himself. But that was my own guilt speaking, the guilt of making choices that would pull him along paths he never asked to walk. In my need to find something, someone to fill the emptiness, I ignored the steady, silent pain in my son's eyes.

Gary's drinking soon turned our life upside down. At first, I tried to keep things together, brushing off his behavior, convincing myself that he was simply "going through a hard time." I made excuses for him, even as his outbursts grew uglier. Nights once filled with laughter turned into tense silences, punctuated by slurred accusations and vicious words. The more I tried to hold onto the man I had once loved, the more he slipped away, leaving behind a person I didn't recognize—a man who was angry, resentful, and unpredictable. And as he changed, so did I. I withdrew from family gatherings, avoided friends, and clung to the hope that things might improve if I just loved him enough.

Adam's resentment grew with each day, and with it, his distance. He watched as I tiptoed around Gary, trying to keep the peace. Once, I caught a look in his eyes that I'll never forget: it was a look of betrayal, hurt, and something else—disappointment. In his eyes, I was no longer his strong, dependable mother. I had become someone else, someone willing to sacrifice herself for the chance at a love that was slipping away. I had hoped Gary would be the balm for the wounds left by my divorce from Stewart. Instead, he was adding more, and it was Adam who felt the sting the most.

One evening, after yet another argument, Gary threw his drink across the room, and it shattered against the wall. Adam, who had been quietly watching from the doorway, stepped between us, his face tight with anger. "Mum, why are you letting him do this?" he asked, his voice trembling. His words struck a nerve, but I couldn't answer him. I couldn't bring myself to admit that I had no idea how to stop the slow unravelling of my life. In my desperation to keep some semblance of love, I had put my son in the shadows. My silence answered him, and he left the room with a look that cut me deeper than any words could.

In the days that followed, I tried to tell myself that Adam was strong, that he would understand one day. But I was lying to myself, clinging to a hope that the damage I was doing to him was somehow temporary. Deep down, I knew that the choices I was making were costing me the relationship with my own son.

One night, as I lay in bed, listening to the sounds of Gary

stumbling through the house, I felt a wave of shame so heavy that I could barely breathe. I thought of Adam, of the young man he was becoming, and I realized I was setting an example that would haunt him. I had allowed Gary's anger, his drinking, his words to poison not only my life but Adam's as well. I wanted to believe that I could fix things, that with enough time, the man I had fallen in love with would return. But it was an illusion, one I could no longer afford to chase. For the sake of my son and for myself, I had to find a way out.

I confided in a friend one afternoon, pouring out the truth of what my life had become. She listened, a sadness in her eyes that made my heart ache, and she told me what I had known all along: "Johanne, you're stronger than this. You deserve better, and so does Adam. You need to choose him—you need to choose yourself."

Her words broke through the fog that had clouded my mind for so long. I couldn't keep sacrificing myself and, most of all, I couldn't keep sacrificing Adam. The guilt of putting Gary before my own son was unbearable, and for the first time, I allowed myself to see the damage I had done. I realized I had been so desperate for love, for something to fill the void, that I had lost sight of what truly mattered.

With a heavy heart, I began to make plans. I saved what little money I could, spoke to a counselor, and finally, one cold morning, I told Gary it was over. He lashed out, as I knew he would, spewing the same venomous words that had once hurt me. But this time, I felt a strange calm, a sense of purpose. I was no longer fighting for him—I was fighting for myself, and for Adam.

I sat down with Adam that same evening, feeling the weight of every decision I had made pressing down on me. He looked at me, his face a mixture of relief and sadness, and for the first time, I spoke openly about the pain, the mistakes, and the regrets that had led us to that moment. "I'm sorry," I whispered, tears blurring my vision. "I know I haven't been the mother you deserved."

He reached across the table, his hand warm and steady. "Mum, I just wanted you to see that you deserved more. That we both did." His words, filled with a strength beyond his years, were like a balm to my wounded heart.

Leaving Gary was the hardest choice I had ever made, but it was also the beginning of my redemption. I had to rebuild not only my life but the trust and love I had nearly lost with my son. Each day brought small steps toward healing, moments where Adam and I laughed together, shared stories, and found a new rhythm. The scars of those years would remain, but they no longer defined us.

Looking back, I see that chapter with a mixture of pain and understanding. My journey had been one marked by missteps and hard lessons, but it had also taught me resilience and the importance of self-worth. I had learned that the love I sought was never worth sacrificing the bond between a mother and her child. And in choosing to walk away, in choosing Adam, I found a strength I never knew I had. The love I had been searching for was there all along, waiting for me to reclaim it. And in the end, I had not only chosen Adam, but I had chosen myself.

Chapter 9: Adam's Rise, A Mother's Pride

Through the turbulent waters of my life—the struggles with Gary, the heartbreak of broken dreams, and the constant uncertainties—one unwavering light continued to shine in my world: my son, Adam. He was my anchor, a source of pride and resilience that gave me strength on even my darkest days. No matter how difficult things became, Adam was a steady reminder of hope and purpose. Watching him grow, despite the challenges he faced, reminded me that the love we shared had carried us through every storm.

From an early age, Adam was different. He possessed an innate compassion and quiet strength that set him apart, a gentle kindness that was rare in a world that often felt harsh. In primary school, he became known as the boy who would protect those who were bullied, standing up for the underdog without a second thought. His teachers would pull me aside to praise his maturity and empathy, calling him "a natural leader." Hearing those words filled me with pride and comforted me through our own trials. Adam's courage was not just a glimpse of who he was as a child but a foreshadowing of the man he would one day become.

As he grew older, Adam took on responsibilities around the house that many children his age never encounter. During my most difficult days, when the weight of life's struggles seemed almost too heavy to bear, he was there—helping with chores, cooking simple meals, and looking after me in quiet, unspoken ways. The pride I felt for him mingled with guilt, knowing he was taking on so much. Yet, even in those moments, I saw a strength in him that was greater than his years.

When Adam reached his teenage years, he developed a passion for learning and a drive to carve his own path. He chose to pursue certificates in groundworks and landscaping at college, a field he loved. I remember the countless nights he would sit at the dining table, poring over his notes, determined to understand every detail. Those were some of my proudest moments. Watching him study with such focus, knowing he was building a foundation for his future, filled me with a fierce pride.

Life at home was difficult, and as he matured, Adam took on even more to help keep things running smoothly. He was a quiet, steadfast support, shouldering burdens that I wished I could take from him. He rarely complained, instead diving headfirst into his coursework and work experience placements with a work ethic that impressed everyone around him. I could see that he wanted to create a better life, one where he could be self-sufficient and proud of his achievements. His resilience and commitment to his future became a powerful example, reminding me to stay strong and focused on my own path forward.

As Adam completed his certificates, he began working with a local landscaping company under the guidance of Chris Myers, a seasoned landscaper who quickly recognized Adam's potential. Working with Chris was a pivotal experience for Adam, one that refined his skills and gave him a solid foundation in the world of landscaping. He learned the intricacies of the trade, from laying patios to tending gardens, and developed a passion for outdoor work. Chris became more than just an employer; he was a mentor, guiding Adam with patience and sharing insights that would shape his future.

Eventually, an opportunity arose that would change everything for him. Adam was offered a position as the site warden on a beautiful caravan park nestled in the Yorkshire Dales. It was a job that combined his love for landscaping with a responsibility for maintaining and caring for the park. The role required a steady hand, a keen eye for detail, and an unwavering commitment—qualities Adam possessed in spades.

The park, surrounded by rolling hills and dales, became his sanctuary. As the site warden, Adam poured himself into his work, taking pride in every task, whether it was mowing the lawns, fixing fences, or tending to the gardens that he made flourish. He found peace in the rhythm of his daily work, and I could see how much he loved being part of something so connected to nature. He spoke about his work with a newfound enthusiasm, describing the beauty of the landscapes he maintained and the satisfaction he felt in creating spaces where people could find peace and happiness.

One evening, as we sat together in our living room, he shared his dreams for the future. "Mum, I want to make a difference with my work," he said, his eyes shining with purpose. "There's something special about taking care of a place that people come to enjoy. It makes me feel like I'm part of something bigger." Hearing him speak with such passion and clarity filled my heart with a mixture of pride and awe. Here was my son, a young man who had faced countless challenges yet emerged with strength, compassion, and a deep sense of purpose.

Through his journey, Adam had not only found a career he loved but also a place that brought him peace. His role as site warden became more than a job; it was a calling, a testament to his resilience and dedication. I knew that he was carving out a life that was his own, a life built on the values he held dear and the strength he had developed through years of perseverance.

In the quiet moments, I often reflected on all that we had been through, on the countless times I worried about the future and wondered if I was giving him the support he needed. But seeing him now, watching him thrive, I knew that every struggle, every hard day, had been worth it. Adam had not only overcome our challenges but had grown into a man with unshakeable integrity, kindness, and a sense of duty that went beyond himself.

His journey became my inspiration. His determination reminded me that no matter the obstacles, we all have the power to rise above, to find joy, and to create a life that reflects who we truly are. He had shown me that resilience wasn't just about enduring but about flourishing, about turning hardship into strength, and using that strength to make a difference in the world.

Looking back, I felt an overwhelming sense of gratitude for the love and bond we shared, a connection that had carried us through the darkest of times and into a future filled with hope and purpose. Adam's journey was a reflection of the values we had built together—a commitment to kindness, to hard work, and to a life lived with integrity. And as I watched him step into his future, I knew that he had become everything I had ever dreamed he would be: a man of courage, compassion, and quiet strength.

Chapter 10: The Battle for My Body

The moment the doctor said the word "cancer," everything in my life changed. I was young, full of energy, and, like anyone at that age, I thought I was invincible. I'd always managed to push through life's challenges, shrugging off fatigue or minor aches, never once thinking they were signs of anything serious. But then came the diagnosis, and it felt as though the ground had been pulled from beneath me. There, in that sterile room with its harsh white lights, I felt my whole world begin to crumble.

Hearing the words out loud was like being hit by a wave of cold reality. "You have cancer." The doctor spoke with the calm, practiced tone of someone who'd delivered the same news to countless others, but for me, it was as if the world had stopped. In that moment, a thousand questions raced through my mind. Why me? Why now? I was just starting to rebuild my life, to find some stability for myself and Adam after all we'd been through. The thought of telling my family, of seeing the pain in their faces, weighed heavily on my heart. I knew this journey was going to be brutal, and I feared for the ones who would have to watch me go through it.

The hardest part was sharing the news with my family. I'll never forget the look on my mother's face as I told her. She'd always been my rock, the person I turned to when everything else was falling apart. But in that moment, I saw her strength waver, her tears flowing freely as she held my hands, squeezing them as if to keep me from slipping away. My father, who had always been so stoic and steady, stood in silence, his face pale, his expression unreadable. Watching their reactions was more painful than any physical symptom I had experienced. It was then that I realized cancer wouldn't just be my battle; it would be theirs as well.

Deborah, my sister, was my anchor throughout. We'd always had a close bond, and as soon as I told her, she was at my side, her support unwavering. She didn't need me to pretend I was okay. One evening, when the weight of it all became too much, I finally broke down, admitting my deepest fear. "Deborah, I'm terrified. What if…" The words caught in my throat, the terror too great to fully voice. She simply held my hand, her gaze steady. "You're a fighter, Johanne. You've survived so much already. We'll get through this." Her strength was a balm to my fractured spirit, and I clung to it like a lifeline.

The first round of treatment was nothing like I had expected. Chemotherapy wasn't just tiring; it was a relentless, all-consuming battle that drained every ounce of energy from my body. I lost weight rapidly, food became tasteless, and I felt sick to my very core. But the worst of it all was the hair loss. I had always taken pride in my long, dark hair, something that felt like a part of me, a part of my identity. Watching it fall out in clumps was like watching pieces of myself disappear, leaving me feeling exposed and vulnerable.

During those early days, mirrors became my enemy. I couldn't bear to look at the stranger staring back at me. Cancer had stripped away so much more than my hair; it had taken my strength, my confidence, my sense of normalcy. I felt like I was disappearing, becoming a shell of the person I once was. But each morning, I forced myself out of bed, one painful step at a time. I'd look at myself, pale and frail, and repeat a silent mantra: You are still here. You are still fighting.

Adam, my dear boy, was a quiet presence during this time. He was older, nearly an adult, and yet his worry was clear in his eyes every time he looked at me. He tried to help in small ways—bringing me water, sitting with me during treatments, offering his silent support. It pained me to see him carry such a burden at his age. I had always wanted to protect him, to shield him from life's hardships. But now, as he shouldered the weight of my illness, I saw a strength in him that both broke and lifted my heart. He was growing up faster than I'd hoped, but his resilience gave me courage.

Throughout the ordeal, friends, family, and even acquaintances became my support network. They rallied around me, sending messages, offering meals, and fundraising to help with the mounting expenses. I felt their love and kindness like a protective shield, bolstering me on the days when I struggled to find strength within myself. On the days when the darkness felt insurmountable, their compassion reminded me that I wasn't alone in this battle. They gave me hope when I had none and, perhaps unknowingly, taught me that love could be a lifeline in times of despair.

I'll never forget the day of my surgery to remove the tumors. It was a gray, overcast morning, and I remember feeling an odd sense of calm mixed with sheer terror as I was wheeled into the operating room. Deborah was there, her hand in mine, whispering words of encouragement as I drifted into unconsciousness. The surgery was long and arduous, but I came through, waking to a haze of pain yet relief. I had survived the first major hurdle, and although I knew the journey was far from over, I felt a small flicker of hope reignite within me.

Recovery was slow, each day a test of patience and resilience. My body, once strong and agile, was now fragile, my energy barely enough to get through simple tasks. But with each small step, I began to regain pieces of myself. I learned to celebrate even the tiniest victories—walking a few steps further, managing a small meal, or simply spending a few minutes outside, feeling the sun on my skin. These moments became milestones, reminders that life was still there, waiting for me to reclaim it.

As I regained my strength, I felt a profound shift within me. The fear that had once dominated my every thought was replaced by a fierce determination to live fully, to savor every moment. Cancer had taken so much, but it had also revealed a resilience I hadn't known existed. It taught me to see life through a new lens, to find joy in the smallest things, and to appreciate the love and support that surrounded me. I knew I would never be the same, and in some ways, I was grateful for that. The battle had scarred me, but it had also given me a new understanding of my own strength.

My family and friends continued to be my pillars throughout the journey, and as I healed, I felt our bonds deepen. The experience had brought us closer in ways that words could hardly describe. We had shared in the fear, the pain, and the triumphs, creating a connection that would forever hold us together. I no longer saw my scars as a reminder of what I had lost; instead, they became symbols of what I had survived, markers of a journey that had made me stronger.

Emerging from that period, I understood that the battle I had faced was more than a fight for my physical health—it was a fight for my identity, my sense of purpose, and my future. I had faced my own mortality and come out on the other side, forever changed. I knew that the shadows would linger, that there would always be moments of fear, but I had found a light within myself that would guide me through any darkness.

Cancer may have left its mark on my body, but it did not define me. It became a part of my story, a chapter that spoke not of defeat, but of resilience and survival. I emerged from that time with a renewed appreciation for life, a fierce love for my family, and an unbreakable spirit. I was no longer just a survivor; I was a warrior, someone who had faced the depths of fear and emerged stronger. The battle for my body had become a testament to my will to live, to love, and to rise above, embracing every scar, every moment, and every breath as a gift.

Chapter 11: Fighting Back Again

Sixteen years had passed since my first fight with cancer, a battle I thought I'd finally left behind. I'd built a life beyond it, allowing myself to believe I'd moved forward, leaving the illness and fear far behind me. But life doesn't always let you close doors so easily. The day I learned that cancer had returned, it felt like the ground had been pulled out from under me. The very world I'd carefully pieced back together began to crumble, leaving me staring into a familiar, terrifying abyss.

The signs crept up gradually. A persistent fatigue that I tried to ignore, small aches I brushed off as part of aging. But deep down, a nagging sense of dread grew. I found myself back in that sterile doctor's office, the same place I'd sat all those years ago at twenty-six, holding Stewart's hand as I was told the unimaginable. Sixteen years had passed, but in that moment, the fear felt as raw as it had back then.

Back then, my first diagnosis had arrived like a bolt from the blue. I'd just turned twenty-six, married to Stewart and starting what I thought would be our life together. I was in the thick of trying to figure out my place in the world, struggling with learning difficulties that made everything harder. To be different had always been my lot, but I'd never expected this.

Cancer felt like a betrayal, as though my own body had turned against me. I remember clinging to Stewart, to my family, to my sister Deborah, as they tried to keep my spirits up and give me strength. And somehow, through the treatments and surgeries, I made it through, with the belief that I had won, that I could close the book on this nightmare and move on.

Now, sixteen years later, facing the same enemy again felt impossible to comprehend. Worse yet, Deborah, my rock, had passed away only months before, after they found a lump that had turned out to be cancer. Losing her left a void that nothing could fill. She had been my confidante, my strength, the one person who understood me in ways no one else ever could. I found myself reeling, without her there to steady me, to whisper the words of encouragement I so desperately needed. I felt stripped bare, and more alone than I'd ever felt.

The doctor's words landed like blows. "We'll need to remove your breasts and ovaries," he said, his voice steady but detached. But I felt it viscerally, the loss hitting me like waves of grief I could barely keep above. My body no longer felt like my own, and I was left questioning what little sense of control I thought I had over my life.

When I told my family, their heartbreak mirrored my own. My mother cried in silence, her pain too deep for words, and my father looked away, his grief etched in every line of his face. The agony of knowing I'd have to put them through this again felt unbearable. How could I ask them to watch me go through this once more, knowing the pain it would bring?

Stewart was gone, but Adam—my son, my pride—was still here. As I faced this new trial, he became my steadfast anchor, even as he struggled to comprehend what was happening. But his resilience, his quiet strength, reminded me that I had a reason to fight, a reason to endure. For him, I would find it in myself to push forward, just as I had before.

The surgeries were brutal, and the recovery was long and painful. Every glance in the mirror was a jarring reminder of all that cancer had taken from me. The scars were raw, angry, each one a stark marker of the battle I had to fight once again. My body felt foreign, a stranger that I had to learn to accept and embrace. But even in those darkest moments, I found an unexpected resilience. The scars, as painful as they were, became symbols of the battles I had fought and survived.

I found a strange solace in creativity, pouring my heart into painting and writing as a way to process the pain, the anger, and the fear. I painted my grief, my rage, and my determination to keep going. With each brushstroke, I reclaimed a piece of myself, chipping away at the darkness that threatened to consume me. Art became my sanctuary, a place where I could be raw and honest without the weight of explanations or expectations.

Some days, the emotional toll felt insurmountable. I found myself longing for the life I'd had before, the days when my greatest worries were the ordinary struggles of life. Cancer's return felt like an uninvited guest, a shadow that tainted everything. But with each passing day, I found new strength. I reached out to support groups, connecting with others who had faced similar battles, each story of survival and resilience adding to my own strength.

My sister Deborah's absence was a wound that never truly healed, but in some ways, I felt her presence. Her memory became a source of courage, her voice echoing in my mind during moments of despair. She had been my rock during my first battle, and now, I felt her guiding me, reminding me of my own strength and resilience. It was as though she were urging me on, whispering, "You've got this, Johanne. Don't give up."

I began to embrace life's simplest joys with a renewed sense of gratitude. I relished the warmth of the sun, the laughter of my family, the peace of a quiet morning. Each day felt like a small victory, a testament to the strength I was reclaiming. Recovery was far from linear—it was filled with setbacks and struggles —but I learned that strength wasn't about the absence of fear; it was about facing it head-on, embracing vulnerability, and allowing others to lift me when I couldn't stand alone.

As I emerged from the depths of treatment and recovery, I understood that cancer had taken many things from me, but it could never take my spirit. I had faced my deepest fears and come out the other side, scarred but stronger. Cancer might have been a part of my story, but it would never define me. I had found a new resilience, a strength forged in the fires of adversity, and as I moved forward, I knew that I would continue to walk this path with courage, grace, and an unbreakable will.

This chapter in my life taught me that resilience is not the absence of hardship but the courage to keep going despite it. Cancer might have cast its shadow, but it would never overshadow the light within me. As I looked to the future, I felt a profound sense of gratitude for each day, knowing that every moment was a gift, and that no battle, no scar, could ever take that away.

Chapter 12: The Power of a Sister's Love

Sisters hold a bond that reaches deep into the soul, one that goes beyond words or understanding, woven from shared laughter, whispered secrets, and a lifetime of standing side by side. For me, that bond was found in Deborah. She was not just my sister but my closest friend, my confidante, the one who could read my heart without my having to say a word. Deborah's love was a light in my life, a steady presence that gave me strength during the most challenging times. Through every trial, her love remained the steady force that kept me moving forward, even when life seemed determined to knock me down.

When I was diagnosed with cancer at twenty-six, Deborah became my lifeline, my rock in a storm of fear and uncertainty. I remember telling her about my diagnosis, expecting tears or anger, maybe even denial. But Deborah, true to herself, didn't falter. She held my hand, her eyes filled with fierce determination. "You're a warrior, Johanne," she said, her voice unshakable. "We're going to face this together, and you're going to come through this stronger." In that moment, her words wrapped around me like armor, and I felt an assurance I hadn't been able to find on my own.

From that moment forward, Deborah was with me at every step. She sat beside me in waiting rooms, her hand in mine, a quiet strength that seemed to seep into my bones. We'd share stories, laugh about childhood memories, and for brief moments, the sterile surroundings of hospital rooms melted away, replaced by the warmth of her presence. She had an uncanny ability to make the darkest moments feel bearable, turning my fears into something manageable, something we could face together.

When the treatments left me feeling weak and weary, Deborah stepped in, her love evident in the small, caring gestures that spoke louder than words. She filled my home with comfort, bringing meals, tidying up, and making sure everything was taken care of. It wasn't just about keeping things running; it was her way of saying, "I'm here. You're not alone." Each dish she prepared, every task she took on, became an expression of her support, a silent promise that she would be there through it all. Deborah's shepherd's pie, in particular, became a staple in my life, a simple meal that warmed more than my body—it nourished my heart, reminding me of the love that surrounded me.

She celebrated every small victory with me, cheering me on with a joy that reminded me of how far we had come together. Whether it was a milestone in my treatment or simply a good day, Deborah made sure to mark each moment, her happiness infectious. We'd laugh, cry, and look to the future, sharing in the hope that our bond would carry us through whatever life threw our way. I often marveled at her strength, at her unwavering belief that I could make it, and in those moments, I found a renewed will to keep fighting.

But life, with its cruel twists, had more in store for us. A few years after my recovery, Deborah fell ill herself. It started with a small lump, one that sent a chill through my spine the moment I heard about it. I watched, helpless, as the roles reversed. Now, it was me sitting by her hospital bed, holding her hand, praying for her recovery. I tried to be the strength for her that she had been for me, but seeing her weakened, fighting her own battle, broke something inside me. Deborah was my foundation, the one who had always lifted me up, and the thought of losing her felt impossible.

The hospital visits became routine, each one more painful than the last. I saw her slipping away, her once-vibrant spirit dimming, though her determination never wavered. She would squeeze my hand, giving me a tired smile, as if to say, "I'm still here, Jo." I held onto those moments, each one a reminder of the love and strength that had defined our relationship. But as the days passed, the hope began to fade, and I was forced to confront the unbearable truth that I was losing her.

When Deborah passed away, it was as if the world shifted, the colors dulled, and the light dimmed. I moved through my days like a ghost, going through the motions, but my heart felt hollow. The laughter we had shared, the comfort of her presence, the knowledge that she would always be there—all of it was gone, leaving a void I couldn't begin to fill. Every memory felt like a knife, cutting deeper into the wound of her absence.

For a long time, I couldn't speak of her. The pain was too raw, the grief too heavy. I avoided our favorite places, the little spots where we'd shared laughter and secrets. Her absence was everywhere, a constant reminder of the love I had lost. I felt unmoored, drifting in a sea of sorrow, struggling to find meaning in a world without her.

But slowly, over time, I began to feel her presence again, not in the physical sense, but in the strength she had left behind in me. Deborah had been my fiercest supporter, my greatest advocate, and as I carried on, I felt her spirit urging me forward, reminding me that her love had not died with her body. It was there, woven into every fiber of my being, a part of who I was and who I would become.

In honoring her memory, I found new purpose. I began volunteering at support groups, sharing my story and lending a hand to others facing their own battles. Every act of kindness, every moment spent helping others, felt like a tribute to Deborah. Her compassion, her courage, her boundless love—all of it lived on through me. I became a storyteller, sharing the lessons she had taught me, using my journey to uplift those who needed a reminder of hope.

In time, I created a memory book filled with photos, letters, and little keepsakes, each one a reminder of the moments we had shared. I would sit with that book on quiet evenings, letting the memories wash over me, feeling her presence in each page. Deborah's spirit became a part of my daily life, a source of strength that I drew on whenever the weight of grief threatened to overwhelm me.

The pain of losing her never truly faded, but I learned to carry it with grace, knowing that her love would always be a part of me. Deborah had taught me that true strength comes not from facing life's battles alone but from embracing the love that surrounds us, from allowing others to lift us when we can't stand on our own. Her legacy was one of kindness, resilience, and an unshakable belief in the power of love.

In the years that followed, I continued to feel her guiding presence. In moments of doubt, I would hear her voice, that familiar tone of encouragement, reminding me that I was capable of overcoming any challenge. She had always believed in me, even when I didn't believe in myself, and that belief became the foundation upon which I built my life.

Deborah's love was a gift that transcended her time on this earth. Her spirit, her strength, her kindness—they live on within me, a testament to the unbreakable bond we shared. Though she may no longer walk beside me, she is a part of everything I do, her love a beacon that lights my way, even in the darkest moments.

In the end, I know that love endures beyond all else. Deborah's love taught me that even in loss, there is a strength that remains, a resilience that carries us forward. She may be gone, but her legacy lives on, a reminder that the power of a sister's love is eternal, a force that neither time nor distance can ever take away.

Chapter 13: Rising from Grief

Grief is unlike any other burden—it's a weight that sinks deep, wrapping around your soul with a force that feels impossible to shake. When my sister Deborah passed away, it was as though the very ground had vanished beneath me, leaving me to drift in a chasm of sorrow that seemed to stretch forever. The world continued to turn around me, but I was frozen in time, caught in a relentless loop of disbelief, trying to comprehend how such a light in my life could be gone. Each day became a battle—to rise from bed, to find purpose, to navigate a life that felt broken beyond repair.

Those first days after her passing blurred together, each one swallowed by the dense fog of heartache and disbelief. My home, once filled with warmth, laughter, and love, felt hollow and cold. Every corner whispered memories of Deborah. I'd find myself drifting into the kitchen, remembering the countless cups of tea we'd shared there, or stepping into the garden where we'd once laughed under the sun. The memories poured over me in waves, each one a bittersweet reminder of the life we had shared, leaving me breathless and clinging to anything that felt real.

At first, I believed that immersing myself in grief was the only way to honor her. The idea of feeling joy again felt like betrayal, like I was leaving her behind. So I clung to the sorrow, letting it fill every moment, thinking that perhaps, if I held on tight enough, I could bring back even a sliver of what we had lost. I would sit in silence, clutching her photograph, whispering into the emptiness, begging for some sign that she was still there. I wasn't just mourning Deborah; I was mourning the world as I had known it, a world that felt irrevocably altered.

Days turned into weeks, and the weeks stretched into months. Slowly, I began to realize that grief, though consuming, wasn't a place to remain—it was a journey, a path I had to walk. Deborah had always encouraged me to face life's storms head-on, to stand strong even in the face of hardship. If I were to truly honor her memory, I needed to carry forward—not by leaving my grief behind, but by transforming it into something that could guide me. Deborah's spirit was too vibrant, too full of love, to let sorrow be her final mark on my life. She would want me to rise, to live fully, to let her legacy be one of love and strength.

My first steps forward were tentative. I started taking early morning walks, letting the cool air fill my lungs, the rhythm of my footsteps grounding me in the present. Nature offered a kind of solace I hadn't anticipated—a reminder that life continued, even in the coldest months. Each tree I passed seemed to tell a story of endurance, standing tall despite the weight of countless winters. Slowly, I began to understand that grief was like winter—a season of cold and darkness, but one that was part of the cycle. And just as nature rebounded with the warmth of spring, I, too, could find light again.

One frosty morning, I paused beneath a towering oak, its branches reaching to the sky. It was scarred and weathered, but still there, still rooted, defying the harshness around it. I felt a surge of kinship with that old tree, as though it were telling me I could endure too. From that moment on, I began to find flickers of strength within myself, a quiet resolve to carry on.

Writing became my sanctuary. Every night, I poured my feelings onto the pages of a journal, giving my grief a voice. I filled those pages with memories of Deborah, with the heartache of her absence and the glimmers of hope I began to feel. Writing allowed me to confront the pain, to shape it into something I could hold, understand, and slowly let go. Through my words, I felt as though I was speaking to her, sharing the journey she could no longer walk with me.

As the months passed, I sought ways to reconnect with the world beyond my sorrow. I began volunteering, supporting those who were facing their own battles with cancer. Through that work, I met people who had endured tremendous loss, their resilience inspiring me to keep moving forward. Their stories were woven with pain and perseverance, threads that, when woven together, formed a tapestry of collective strength. I realized that in helping others, I was also healing myself.

One day, I met Rachel, a woman who, like me, had lost a sister to illness. We sat in a small café, sharing stories, and in her eyes, I saw the same pain that had shadowed my own. She spoke of her sister with a mixture of sadness and joy, her words resonating with a profound understanding. Over time, Rachel became a dear friend, a companion in my journey through grief. Through her, I rediscovered the warmth of connection, the laughter that Deborah and I had shared. We supported one another, our friendship a lifeline that brought comfort, reminding me that it was okay to smile again, to remember our sisters with love instead of sorrow.

Gradually, I allowed myself to feel happiness in small, precious moments. I would sit in the garden, letting the warmth of the sun touch my skin, relishing in the simple beauty of the world. I found myself laughing, a quiet sound that felt foreign at first, but soon became a new expression of the love I still held for Deborah. I began to understand that joy and sorrow could coexist, that one didn't diminish the other. Loving Deborah meant living fully, holding her memory close as I embraced the life I still had to live.

There were days, of course, when grief would resurface with

a force that took me by surprise. I would feel the familiar ache, the emptiness that came with longing for one more conversation, one more hug. But even in those moments, I felt a quiet resilience within me, a strength I hadn't known I possessed. I learned to carry my grief with grace, to let it be a part of me without letting it consume me.

Eventually, I began sharing my story, speaking at support groups and gatherings, hoping to offer others a glimmer of hope. Each time I spoke, I felt closer to Deborah, as if her spirit was with me, guiding my words, lending me courage. My vulnerability became my strength, a bridge that connected me to others who were also finding their way through loss. Through those moments, I understood that Deborah's legacy was not confined to my memories of her; it lived on in the lives she touched, in the love that continued to ripple outward.

In time, I found that rising from grief was not about leaving Deborah behind; it was about carrying her forward, allowing her spirit to shape my journey. She had always been my strength, my inspiration, and even in her absence, she remained my guiding light. I learned to find beauty in the world once more, to cherish the memories we had shared, and to celebrate her life through mine.

Now, as I reflect on the journey of grief and healing, I understand that it's a lifelong process. Grief does not fade; it transforms, becoming a quiet companion that walks beside us. But through that journey, I have found resilience, love, and a deeper understanding of what it means to live fully. Deborah's memory continues to inspire me to embrace life with open arms, to be kind, and to live with purpose. Her love has become my foundation, a strength that endures beyond the boundaries of time.

Rising from grief has shown me that though life is marked by loss, it is also filled with love. And with every step I take, I carry Deborah with me, forever my sister, forever my strength. She is a part of everything I do, a presence that fills my heart and lights my way, a testament to the unbreakable bond we shared. And as long as I live, her spirit will continue to shine, a beacon of love that neither distance nor death can ever take away.

Chapter 14: My Silent World

In life, sound becomes a familiar, invisible presence—laughter, voices, the melody of daily routines, grounding us in our existence. For years, these sounds filled my world, enriching it in ways I took for granted. But by my thirties, my world began to shift, and what I once knew slipped away, bit by bit, into silence. This silent world wasn't one I chose, but it was one I'd come to inhabit as hearing loss slowly closed in, reshaping my life and forcing me to find a new rhythm.

The first signs crept in quietly. At first, they were easy to overlook, just a few missed words, moments when a conversation seemed to slip through my grasp. I would find myself nodding along, pretending I'd heard, laughing when others laughed even if I'd missed the punchline. And as time went on, gatherings became harder, full of voices that seemed distant and unreachable. It felt like being on the outside, watching everyone through a thick pane of glass. As the silence grew, so did my isolation, and eventually, I knew something deeper was happening.

When I finally sat in the doctor's office, listening as he explained the reality of my diagnosis, it felt like the world was folding in on me. There was no escape. I had known it was coming, yet nothing prepared me for the finality of his words: "Your hearing will continue to deteriorate." In that sterile room, I felt the weight of those words settle on me, an unwanted companion. My future stretched ahead of me, shadowed by uncertainty and a quiet I wasn't ready for. What would this mean for my relationships, my connection to the world, to myself?

For a time, I refused to accept it. I carried on, clinging to the sounds that remained, pretending this was just a phase. But as sounds continued slipping away, my world shrank. It wasn't just the loss of noise—it was the gradual distancing from people I loved, from conversations, from the joy of shared laughter. I began to fear social gatherings, hating the moments when I'd miss the flow of conversation, feeling trapped in an invisible shell, alone in a crowd.

I knew I needed help, and so I tried hearing aids. The first time I put them on, the world burst into sound, almost violently so. Even the quiet creak of the floor, the faint hum of distant machinery, felt like an assault. Every sound was magnified, raw and unfiltered. I had expected relief, but instead, I felt disoriented and vulnerable. These hearing aids were a bridge back to the world, but they were also a visible mark of my struggle, a reminder of the growing gap between the person I had been and the one I was becoming. In a way, I grieved for that past self, for the ease of communication, for the simplicity of sound.

Wearing hearing aids meant adapting. I had to learn to rely on more than just sound—I had to watch lips, observe facial expressions, interpret gestures. Every conversation became a tightrope walk of concentration and patience, requiring me to focus with an intensity that was exhausting. I would catch myself nodding politely, hoping I'd grasped the right meaning, and then the frustration would rise, thick and painful, a reminder of what I had lost. In this new reality, I felt as though I straddled two worlds: one, noisy and familiar but out of reach; the other, silent and alien but undeniable.

Gradually, the emotional toll of this silent world seeped into every part of my life. I found myself retreating, unwilling to face the loneliness that grew with each missed word, each conversation lost. I watched my family and friends laugh together, unable to join in, and the silence within me deepened. For a time, it felt unbearable, an isolation I could never explain, and the weight of it threatened to overwhelm me. But in the depths of this struggle, I found a glimmer of hope in a support group for those with hearing loss.

In that community, I found others who understood. There,

we shared stories of frustration, strategies for coping, moments of connection. It was the first time I felt seen in a world where I'd been invisible. Our shared silence became a bridge, connecting us in ways I hadn't anticipated. They understood the subtle pains, the missed nuances, and the ache of isolation. Through these friendships, I began to reshape my relationship with my hearing loss. I wasn't alone in my struggle; I was part of a resilient community, one that had found ways to live fully, to find meaning despite the silence.

With time, I found courage in advocating for myself, asking people to look at me when they spoke, to slow down, to allow me the chance to understand. At first, the vulnerability felt raw, but then it transformed into a quiet strength. I began to see my hearing aids not as symbols of defeat but as tools that allowed me to engage with the world on my terms. And as I navigated each interaction with this newfound openness, I learned that people were more understanding than I had feared.

There were still overwhelming moments, of course. Family gatherings or dinners in noisy places often felt like a sensory avalanche, the sounds colliding in a chaotic blend that made me long for silence. I'd step away, seeking out quiet spaces, letting myself breathe. In honoring my needs, I found peace, a reminder that I could shape this silent world in a way that allowed me to thrive, even if it meant stepping away from the clamor.

In the midst of these challenges, I found unexpected beauty. I savored the sounds I could still hear: the laughter of my son, Adam, the soft rustling of the breeze through leaves, the simple hum of life around me. Every sound became precious, each one a reminder of my connection to the world. And in those quiet spaces, I found a new appreciation for nonverbal communication. I learned to watch body language, to recognize the warmth in someone's gaze, to cherish the meaning in a shared smile or gentle touch. Words weren't the only form of connection; I could still feel love, kindness, empathy, and joy even when they were silent.

Reflecting on this journey, I realized that hearing loss is only one part of my life's story. It has taught me resilience, empathy, and the beauty of connection that goes beyond words. In my silent world, I have found strength in vulnerability, learning that asking for help and showing my true self is not weakness but a sign of courage. I see my hearing loss not as an end, but as another layer of the person I am, a depth of experience that has enriched my life.

Moving forward, I carry the lessons of my silent world with me. Life, I have learned, is filled with moments of both sound and silence, and each holds its own unique power. In my silent world, I've discovered that we can still be heard, still make a difference, still find joy. With every step, I remind myself that life's symphony includes both sound and stillness, each adding its own beauty to my journey.

I may not hear the world as others do, but I have found a way to listen deeply, to embrace the quiet, and to live fully, creating a world that resonates in my heart, a melody that is mine alone.

Chapter 15: Scarred but Beautiful

Life imprints itself on us in ways we often can't see coming, but the evidence remains—etched on our hearts and sometimes, unmistakably, on our bodies. For me, those marks became painfully visible, and every inch of skin touched by a surgeon's knife told a story I hadn't chosen to tell. The scars from my mastectomy were raw and unyielding reminders of a battle fought without my consent, a journey into loss that demanded more strength than I'd ever imagined. In the beginning, I avoided mirrors, and when I caught an accidental glimpse, my body no longer felt like my own. Yet, as time passed, those scars transformed from painful reminders into profound symbols, not of brokenness, but of resilience. I became someone who bore the weight of survival like a warrior who has weathered every storm and learned to find peace in the scars left behind.

When the surgeon first explained the necessity of a mastectomy, his voice was calm and his words clinical, but for me, they were thunderous, echoing with a finality that chilled me to the core. Losing my breasts wasn't merely physical; it was a disorientation that rattled my identity. For years, my body had been a trusted vessel, sturdy and whole. Now, that vessel felt cracked, and the idea of it enduring this irrevocable change was like staring down the edge of a cliff. I remember lying awake in the small hours of the morning, feeling the ache of fear deep in my bones, wondering if I could ever feel like myself again.

The aftermath of the surgery was a blur of emotions I could hardly name, let alone manage. My first look at the scars brought a fresh wave of anguish. They were stark and angry, red lines marking the places I had been cut, both physically and emotionally. Each time I looked, the scars seemed to taunt me, reminding me of what was gone. I felt as though I had lost a part of my femininity, of what made me whole. I couldn't dress without feeling a pang of loss, each garment slipping over skin that no longer felt like mine, covering a body I barely recognized.

Grief settled over me like a dense fog, infiltrating every part of my life. The woman I once knew, the one who carried herself with ease and pride, seemed to fade into the background, replaced by someone I could hardly look at in the mirror. I began to withdraw, ashamed and wary of letting others see my pain. I was determined not to burden those I loved, but that silence only deepened the isolation, feeding the quiet despair that had taken root. My scars weren't just on my skin; they ran deeper, weaving themselves into my very sense of self.

Months passed, and though the physical pain lessened, the emotional wounds remained fresh, raw as the day I'd first looked at myself post-surgery. Yet somewhere along the way, a quiet shift began. It started with a single thought—that perhaps these scars didn't signify a brokenness, but a survival. They weren't simply evidence of loss; they were evidence of life, of a fight I hadn't wanted but had faced all the same. My body, once smooth and whole, was now marked by a fierce resilience I hadn't realized I possessed. Slowly, I began to let go of the idea that these scars diminished me. Instead, I started to wonder if they could, in their way, make me whole.

One day, while browsing the internet, I came across images of women who had chosen to transform their mastectomy scars into art. They had tattooed over the scars, using designs that not only covered the evidence of their surgeries but embraced it, turning something painful into something breathtakingly beautiful. They weren't hiding; they were celebrating. I was transfixed. Could I, too, reclaim my body in this way? Could I wear my scars proudly, not as a source of shame but as a badge of courage?

The idea took root in me, growing with every day. I began sketching designs, pouring over ideas that might reflect my journey. Eventually, I settled on a lotus flower, a symbol that resonated deeply within me. The lotus blooms in

muddy water, rising above the murk to display its beauty—
a perfect metaphor for the resilience I had found through my
ordeal. I wanted that image on my body, a visual reminder
of the strength I had discovered within myself.

When I arrived at the tattoo parlor, a mixture of nerves and
exhilaration washed over me. Sitting in the chair, waiting for the
artist to begin, I felt vulnerable but ready. Each prick of the needle
felt strangely liberating, a release of the pain I had carried since
the surgery. I watched, entranced, as the ink formed lines and
curves that transformed my scars into a vibrant, beautiful lotus.
I felt as though I were shedding an old layer of myself, finally
letting go of the woman I had mourned and embracing the one
who had survived. When the tattoo was finished, I looked in the
mirror, and for the first time, I saw beauty reflected back at me.

In the weeks that followed, I became bolder. My tattoo became a
source of pride, a way to share my journey with others. I began
to tell my story, not hiding my scars but showing them, knowing
that I wasn't alone in this experience. I connected with other
women who had faced similar battles, each of us finding strength
in our shared resilience. The lotus on my chest became a bridge,
allowing me to reach out to those who had walked this road,
each of us carrying scars that spoke of courage and survival.

Through this journey, I found that beauty wasn't about
perfection or flawlessness; it was about the stories etched
into our skin, the battles we survived, and the grace we
discovered in ourselves along the way. My scars no longer felt
like limitations but parts of my identity that enriched me,
that told of a strength I had found when I needed it most.

Life is rarely as neat or as kind as we wish, and often we are left
to carry burdens we never asked for. But through it all, I've come
to understand that beauty doesn't lie in untouched skin or a life
free of hardship. It lies in the resilience that scars reveal, the way

they whisper of pain transformed into strength. My scars, once a source of pain, are now part of what makes me whole. They speak of survival, of endurance, of the ability to rise again.

Today, I look at my scars and feel a deep, unwavering pride. I am scarred but beautiful, whole not because I returned to who I once was, but because I embraced the woman I became. Each line etched into my skin is a testament to the battles I've fought and the resilience I've discovered within me. My scars are a reminder that life may leave its marks, but those marks can be as beautiful as the strength that carried me through.

As I continue my journey, I hold onto the knowledge that beauty is found in resilience, in the strength to rise despite hardship. And with each step forward, I carry my scars as symbols of hope, knowing that I am scarred but beautiful —whole, not in spite of my journey, but because of it.

Chapter 16: Family Bonds

Family is the kind of blessing you don't always realize the depth of until life throws you into the storms, leaving you reaching for any solid ground. For me, my family has been that anchor, the foundation on which I've built my life and found my strength. Looking back, I'm filled with gratitude for the love that surrounded me, the unwavering support of my parents, Ted and Dena, and the resilience we shared. In every trial, every moment of heartache, they were the ones who reminded me that no matter what life took away, I was never alone.

Growing up in the quiet village of Silsden, our family's life was simple but rich with meaning. Our home was warm, filled with laughter and the sweet scent of my mother's baking. Ted and Dena instilled in us the importance of kindness, resilience, and honesty. My father's steady presence was a constant reassurance, while my mother's gentle strength wrapped around us like a cozy blanket. They were the kind of parents who showed their love in the everyday moments: a quiet word of encouragement, a shared meal, or the way they'd sit with us and listen, really listen, as if our little worries mattered as much as the world's troubles.

My mother, Dena, was the heart of our home. She was gentle but unyielding, the kind of woman who had a knack for making everything feel right. In moments of doubt, I could always turn to her. Whether it was a school struggle, the sting of rejection, or the uncertainty of adulthood, her words were a balm to my soul. She'd listen to my troubles, her face filled with empathy, and somehow, with just a few words, she'd help me see my strength. "You're made of strong stuff, love," she'd say, with a smile that held a quiet knowing. Her love taught me resilience, and her wisdom became a source of strength I'd draw on throughout my life.

My father, Ted, was our anchor. Quiet and unassuming, he was the kind of man who believed that strength was shown in actions, not words. He didn't need to say much to let us know how deeply he cared. If ever we were in trouble, he was there, no questions asked, his presence a steady reminder that, no matter what, we had someone in our corner. Ted believed in the importance of integrity, a lesson he lived every day and one he instilled in me from a young age. "Always be true to yourself," he'd say. "Hold your head high, and don't let anyone make you feel small." Those words became a compass, guiding me through the years, grounding me when life felt uncertain.

As I grew older, I came to cherish these moments with my parents, realizing how much of who I was came from them. They were my constant support, my cheerleaders in every endeavor. Through every challenge—whether it was the rocky road of single motherhood or my battle with cancer—they were by my side. I knew that no matter what storms I faced, my parents would always be there, their unwavering love a steady force that held me together.

My relationship with my brother, Mark, was complex. Growing up, we shared a typical sibling relationship, full of laughter, teasing, and the occasional spat. But as we moved into adulthood, Mark became more reserved, retreating into his own world. I often wished we were closer, that we could share the same bond I had with Deborah, our sister. I knew Mark cared deeply in his own quiet way, but he was guarded, protective of his heart. There were times I felt frustrated, yearning for the kind of connection that comes easily to some siblings. But as the years passed, I learned to accept him as he was, understanding that love can be expressed in countless ways.

When Deborah passed away, it was like a shadow fell over us all. Her absence was a hole we each felt in our own way, a wound that would never fully heal. In the wake of her loss, I felt an urge to reach out to Mark, hoping that we could support each other through our grief. We began to talk more, sharing memories of Deborah, laughing and crying together. Talking about her was painful but cathartic, a way to keep her spirit alive in our lives. Those conversations brought us closer, allowing us to navigate the complexity of our grief together, even if we did so in different ways. It was a reminder that family ties, no matter how strained, have a strength all their own.

Our shared memories of Deborah became a bridge between us. Despite our differences, I realized that my relationship with Mark was its own kind of connection—a bond that didn't need constant communication to be felt. We were bound by our shared history, by the love we held for our family, and by the experiences that shaped us. Sibling relationships aren't always easy; they're filled with their own ups and downs, shaped by time, distance, and the lives we each carve out. But they are a part of who we are, and I learned to value my bond with Mark, knowing that he, too, was a part of the family I cherished so deeply.

Family gatherings became a source of solace, a way to reconnect and celebrate the love we shared. Sunday lunches at my parents' house or evenings spent chatting over cups of tea became sacred moments, each one a reminder of the roots that bound us together. I cherished these times with my parents, seeing in them the pillars of our family. I found joy in reconnecting with Mark, feeling flashes of the brother I had known in childhood, and realizing that our bond, though sometimes quiet, was unbreakable. Our family gatherings became a celebration of resilience, a reminder that no matter what life threw at us, we would always have each other.

In my parents, I saw the strength and love that had carried us through life's hardest moments. In Mark, I found a brother who understood, even in silence, the journey we'd all walked. Our family connection became a sanctuary, a source of comfort and joy, grounding me in a world that sometimes felt chaotic and unpredictable. As I looked around at my family, I felt a deep sense of gratitude for the love that had shaped me, for the bonds that held us together, and for the knowledge that, no matter what, we were forever connected.

As I continue on my journey, I carry with me the love and wisdom my family has given me. Our family bonds are a testament to resilience, compassion, and an enduring strength that guides me through each chapter of my life. In moments of quiet reflection, I am filled with gratitude for the family that has always believed in me, for the love that has been my compass, and for the strength that keeps me moving forward.

Our journey as a family has been filled with its own challenges, but it has been one of love, forgiveness, and understanding. It is a love I carry with me every day, a foundation that has made me who I am and a legacy that I hope to pass on. No matter where life takes us, I know that our hearts are forever connected, bound by a love that is as resilient as it is unconditional.

Chapter 17: Transforming My Life

Life has an uncanny way of guiding us toward change, sometimes through whispers and at other times through profound upheavals that leave us no choice but to confront ourselves. I had buried pain and hardship beneath layers of resilience, letting the scars of grief, illness, and struggle accumulate like silent weights within me. By the time I reached my late fifties, these burdens had settled heavily on my body and spirit. I knew, in the stillness of one quiet afternoon, that if I was to reignite the light within me, I'd need to confront these shadows and step into a new chapter.

That decision—born from a place of necessity, perhaps even desperation—felt monumental. It wasn't just about appearance or fitness, but about reclaiming pieces of myself I had thought were lost. Years of battling through illness, loss, and the relentless grind of life had dulled my spirit. I wanted to heal not only my body but also my heart, to release the weight of all I had carried and rediscover the vibrant woman I once knew. Change was no longer a choice but a promise I made to myself.

My journey began with the simplest of steps. Walking became my daily ritual, each footfall a quiet commitment to the future I was creating. At first, my steps were slow, each one labored under the weight of both physical strain and emotional burden. But as the days passed, the movements felt more natural, like a sacred rhythm that restored me. I found peace in the feel of the cool breeze against my skin, the crunch of gravel beneath my feet, the morning sun warming my face. Each walk was an affirmation that I could keep moving forward, even on the days when my spirit felt tired.

Soon, I recognized that this transformation was more than physical; I had to confront the habits and patterns that had kept me tethered to an old way of living. For years, I'd used food as comfort, a temporary balm to soothe the ache of loneliness or loss. But as I took control of my life, I began to see food as something different—as nourishment, not escape. I filled my kitchen with fresh, colorful ingredients, savoring the simple pleasure of creating meals that truly fueled me. Each meal became a form of self-care, a small victory that affirmed I was worthy of attention and love.

The journey was not without struggle. Old habits die hard, and there were days when my mind whispered doubts, coaxing me back into familiar routines. But I reminded myself of the woman I was working so hard to become—the woman who stood tall, unburdened by the ghosts of her past, living a life full of vibrancy and purpose. I learned to be patient with myself, allowing for setbacks and celebrating even the smallest steps forward. In each slip, I found a lesson, something that propelled me back onto my path with renewed resolve.

As my body grew stronger, I began to feel lighter in spirit, too. The weight I had carried for years, both inside and out, seemed to melt away. I looked in the mirror and saw not just a smaller figure but a woman reclaiming her own identity. I no longer shied away from my reflection, no longer felt ashamed of my imperfections. Instead, I felt pride in my body's strength, in the resilience that had carried me through every battle. I started to see the changes as more than skin-deep; they were symbols of my commitment to myself, a promise kept, a journey embraced.

Community became a powerful ally in my transformation. I joined fitness groups and support networks, places where I met people who, like me, were on their own journeys to renewal. We shared our struggles, celebrated each other's victories, and held each other up through the challenging days. These connections reminded me that I wasn't alone. We became a chorus of resilience, cheering each other on and finding strength in our shared commitment to change. It was in these friendships that I found the motivation to keep going, to keep growing, knowing that we were all in this together.

As the weeks turned into months, I noticed a profound shift in my mind. I started practicing mindfulness and meditation, giving myself the gift of stillness each day. In the quiet, I learned to listen to my own needs, to recognize the patterns of thought that had held me captive for so long. I found joy in the present moment, letting go of the need for perfection, and embracing the beauty of simply being. Each breath became a release, a letting go of years of stress and worry, and in their place, I found a peace I hadn't known was possible.

Embracing this transformation, I became my own advocate. I took charge of my health, scheduling regular checkups, asking questions, and educating myself about my body's needs. The empowerment I felt from this was immense. No longer a passive participant in my own life, I was actively shaping my future, making choices rooted in self-care and love. I was rewriting my story, and in each step, I felt myself growing stronger, more resilient, and more determined to live fully.

Looking back, I see that this journey was about much more than physical change. It was a journey into my own soul, a path to uncovering resilience I never knew I had. I am not just a survivor of life's hardships; I am a warrior, shaped by every struggle and every triumph. This journey has taught me to honor myself, to recognize the beauty in perseverance, and to celebrate every small victory. Transformation, I've learned, is not a destination; it's a commitment to ongoing growth, to nurturing a life filled with purpose, joy, and vitality.

Today, I look to the future with hope and possibility. I feel a deep calling to share my story with others, to inspire those who feel trapped by their past or by the weight of their struggles. I want them to know that transformation is possible, that it's never too late to reclaim your life and step into a brighter future. This mission fills me with a passion I've never known, a desire to be a beacon for those who are just beginning their journeys.

In transforming my life, I have discovered a love for myself that is rooted in resilience, strength, and the belief that we are all capable of profound change. I have learned to embrace my imperfections, to find beauty in my scars, and to celebrate the journey rather than the destination. With each day, I carry forward the understanding that our challenges do not define us—it is our response to them that shapes who we are. And I am determined to become someone worthy of this journey, a woman who stands tall, unapologetically embracing the life she has fought to create.

As I walk this path, I do so with gratitude for every lesson, every challenge, and every victory. I am scarred, but I am beautiful, strong in my imperfections, and hopeful in my journey. Life, with all its trials, has become my teacher, and in embracing its lessons, I have found a joy that transcends the ordinary. I am free, renewed, and filled with the unshakable belief that we are all capable of transforming our lives into something extraordinary.

Chapter 18: Resilience in Every Breath

The morning sun streams through my living room window, filling the space with a gentle warmth, its light pooling across the floor like an embrace. I close my eyes and breathe deeply, feeling that warmth settle within, a reminder of the strength that has brought me to this point. This home, now filled with echoes of my journey, has become my sanctuary—a place where I celebrate my resilience and honor every scar, every lesson, and every triumph. I have faced more than my share of trials and heartbreak, and yet, as I sit here, I am at peace.

For a long time, the idea of living alone felt daunting, almost impossible. I worried that the silence would amplify every hardship, that solitude would feel like a heavy cloak. But this chapter of my life, marked by quiet solitude, has surprised me. It has been transformative in ways I never anticipated. My loyal companion, Mylo—a mischievous, green-eyed tabby with a knack for stealing my pens and curling up in the sunniest spots —has been a source of comfort, his quiet, steadfast presence reminding me daily that love often arrives in the simplest forms. Mylo and I have found our own rhythm, a gentle companionship that makes even the quietest moments feel full.

Looking back on the path that brought me here, I feel an immense gratitude for the resilience I've discovered within myself. Each scar, each laugh line, every tear shed in solitude, and every hand held in sorrow or joy—they are all woven into the tapestry of my life. My son, Adam, my parents, Ted and Dena, and my late sister, Deborah, are as much a part of that fabric as my own struggles. Their love and strength have carried me through the darkest moments when I couldn't carry myself. Adam's journey inspires me daily; his quiet resolve serves as a beacon, reminding me of the resilience that runs deep within our family. My parents' presence, steady and unwavering, has taught me what it means to love unconditionally and to stand strong through any storm.

The adjustment to life alone brought its challenges, and in the beginning, the silence felt like a weight pressing down on me. It was as if the quiet itself carried the echoes of all that I had lost and the burdens I still held. But as days turned into weeks, I found a rhythm all my own. I began to see solitude not as a void but as an opportunity—a chance to reconnect with parts of myself I had long buried under years of caring for others and weathering life's storms. Living alone became, not a trial, but a canvas on which I could paint a life that was purely, authentically mine.

In this space, I've cultivated routines that bring me both comfort and joy. Mornings begin with a warm cup of tea, a few pages of journaling, and the soft presence of Mylo, who curls up beside me, his quiet purring like a lullaby for my soul. Journaling, a habit I started during my cancer treatments, has become a sacred ritual. Each entry is a testament to my journey, capturing the highs, the lows, and the victories that fill my days. Through these words, I've come to honor the woman I've become, to see the beauty in the resilience that defines her.

Mylo, with his soft fur and playful spirit, is a daily reminder of the simplicity and joy that life still offers. He brings light into my home with his little antics, chasing sunbeams across the floor or playfully pawing at the edge of my book. His companionship has softened the edges of my solitude, his quiet loyalty a reminder that love is often found in the smallest gestures. Together, we sit by the window and watch the world pass by, our lives intertwined in a harmony I hadn't known I needed.

Living alone has also deepened my appreciation for the relationships that matter most. My parents, Ted and Dena, remain pillars of strength and wisdom, and our weekly visits are filled with laughter, stories, and the comfort of shared love. My brother and I, despite our differences, have found a new closeness, an understanding that transcends words. Family, I've come to realize, isn't defined by proximity but by love that endures, love that shows up, unwavering and constant, even in the hardest of times.

In these quiet moments of reflection, I've come to understand that resilience isn't merely about surviving hardship. It's about finding beauty within it, about embracing each challenge with an open heart. Resilience is the quiet choice to keep going, to believe in the future, even when the path is unclear. Each breath I take feels like a victory, a reminder that I am still here, still standing, and still filled with the courage to face whatever comes next.

As I look to the future, I feel an unexpected desire to share my story, to reach out to others who may be walking their own paths of hardship and healing. I want to create a space where people can gather, share their experiences, and find strength in one another's resilience. My journey, once marked by isolation and pain, has become a beacon of hope, a light I wish to share with those who may feel lost. I want to remind them that healing is possible, that within each of us lies the strength to overcome even the deepest wounds.

Through this journey, I have learned that resilience is as much about letting go as it is about holding on. I've let go of parts of my story that no longer serve me, embracing instead the scars that remain. These scars, once painful reminders of loss, have become symbols of survival, proof that I am whole, not despite my hardships, but because of them. They are etched in my skin, in my heart, and they tell a story that is uniquely mine.

A deep peace fills me now. The woman I see in the mirror is no longer merely a survivor—she is someone who has chosen to celebrate life, to embrace every challenge as an opportunity for growth. I carry with me the strength of my loved ones, the wisdom of my journey, and the quiet companionship of Mylo, who watches over me with the same steadfast loyalty I find within myself. This journey, once filled with sorrow and struggle, has transformed into a celebration of resilience, of life's quiet, powerful beauty.

This isn't the end of my story; it's the beginning of a new chapter. I carry my scars with pride, my resilience with gratitude, and my heart with hope. I am ready for whatever lies ahead, for each twist and turn, knowing I have the strength to face it all. My life, though marked by hardship, is filled with love, with purpose, and with a joy that is quiet yet unbreakable. And as I move forward, I do so with the unshakable knowledge that, in every breath, I carry the power of transformation within me.

Final Thoughts

As I reach this moment, drawing together the threads of my life's journey, I'm struck by how each chapter, each lesson, has shaped and refined the person I am today. The path has been winding, often steep and thorny, but it's been mine alone, and for that, I am deeply grateful. In every joy and heartbreak, every struggle and victory, I see the mosaic of a life fully lived—a life that has, at its core, been about resilience, about rising again and again, even when the world seemed bent on keeping me down.

The trials I've faced have been numerous, each with a weight that felt impossible to bear at times. Yet here I am, on the other side, having emerged not unscathed, but undeniably stronger. Through it all, I have discovered that resilience isn't simply enduring hardship; it's finding a way to thrive despite it, to embrace life's unpredictable nature with a spirit that remains unbroken. Every challenge I faced refined me, peeling away layers of fear and self-doubt, revealing a strength I hadn't known lay within me all along.

The love and support of my family, especially the guiding presence of my parents, Ted and Dena, the memory of my sister, Deborah, and the courage of my son, Adam, were lights along the way. Their belief in me held me together when I felt like crumbling, their encouragement urging me forward even in my darkest hours. And to my dear friend, Mr. Karl Emsley, I owe a debt of gratitude that words cannot fully capture. Karl's unwavering faith in my story, his steady encouragement, and his quiet but powerful belief in my voice made this book possible. His friendship has been a cornerstone of strength, and I count myself fortunate beyond measure to have had his support.

My journey has taught me that the scars we bear—whether on our bodies or in our hearts—are not marks of defeat. They are symbols of endurance, of battles fought and won, reminders that we are stronger than we sometimes believe. Life, with its unpredictable twists and turns, has taken me to places I never expected, forcing me to confront truths I once tried to ignore. But through each test, I have found my way forward, discovering that true resilience lies not in the absence of struggle, but in the grace with which we choose to move beyond it.

The story I leave here is one of survival, yes, but also one of transformation. It's a testament to the beauty found in imperfection, in rising from the ashes of sorrow to embrace joy, in finding strength in places I thought barren. In learning to live with learning difficulties, in embracing the parts of me that others might call "different," I've found a unique kind of freedom. I now see that these differences, these struggles, are not limitations; they are gifts that have taught me empathy, patience, and the unshakeable power of self-belief.

To anyone who reads these words, I hope my journey offers you a flicker of hope, a reminder that, no matter how heavy life's burdens may seem, there is always a path forward. Life can be harsh and unkind, but within each of us is a strength that can bend but not break. In our resilience lies our truest beauty—the ability to rise from hardship, to shape our stories with courage, and to embrace ourselves fully, scars and all.

As I close this chapter, I carry with me a heart brimming with gratitude and a spirit that feels whole. This is not an ending; it's a continuation—a promise to myself to live each day with intention, to honor the resilience I have found, and to face the future with hope and a willingness to grow. Life, in all its complexity, is beautiful. And as I step forward, I do so with the knowledge that every breath, every heartbeat, carries within it the story of a life well-lived, a life that celebrates resilience in every form.

Thank you, Mr. Karl Emsley, my dear friend, for walking this path with me, for believing in me and this book, and for showing me that every story deserves to be told. You have been my steady light, my anchor, and my friend, and I am forever grateful for your unwavering presence.

And to all who read this, may you find within these pages a spark to nurture your own resilience, to face each new day with courage and grace. Life's challenges may be many, but in the end, we are more powerful than we ever imagined. So live fully, love fiercely, and, above all, believe in your strength, for that is the essence of resilience—the greatest gift we can give to ourselves and the world.

Recommended Reading

If my story has inspired you, consider these books that delve into resilience, overcoming life's challenges, and finding inner strength:

"Option B: Facing Adversity, Building Resilience, and Finding Joy"

By Sheryl Sandberg and Adam Grant

Sheryl Sandberg's personal account of loss and resilience, written with psychologist Adam Grant, offers insights into healing after tragedy. The book explores how to rediscover joy and strength in life's darkest moments.

"When Breath Becomes Air"

By Paul Kalanithi

This memoir by a neurosurgeon facing terminal cancer beautifully captures the struggle for purpose and identity in the face of life-altering challenges, reflecting themes similar to those Johanne has faced.

"Man's Search for Meaning"

By Viktor E. Frankl

Psychiatrist Viktor Frankl recounts his experiences as a Holocaust survivor, providing a powerful perspective on finding meaning amidst suffering, a core message in Johanne's journey.

"The Choice: Embrace the Possible"

By Dr. Edith Eva Eger

Dr. Eger's story of survival and healing after the Holocaust speaks to the power of resilience, love, and the choices that shape our lives, offering deep lessons in overcoming past traumas.

Thank You for Reading

Thank you for taking the time to walk this journey with me through the pages of my book. Sharing my story—its joys, heartbreaks, and the resilience I found along the way—has been a deeply personal and healing experience. I hope that my experiences have offered you comfort, inspiration, or simply the reminder that, no matter how difficult life becomes, there is always a way forward.

Your willingness to listen, to feel, and to understand has brought my story to life in a way I could only have dreamed of. Remember, we are all stronger than we think, braver than we feel, and more resilient than we know. May this book remind you to hold onto hope, to trust in your own strength, and to keep going, one day at a time.

With all my gratitude,

Johanne Roberts

Printed in Great Britain
by Amazon

50042287R00056